Reflections From the Quiet Corner

Reflections From the Quiet Corner

Bruce Howard

XULON PRESS

Xulon Press
2301 Lucien Way #415
Maitland, FL 32751
407.339.4217
www.xulonpress.com

© 2021 by Bruce Howard

All rights reserved solely by the author. The author guarantees all contents are original and do not infringe upon the legal rights of any other person or work. No part of this book may be reproduced in any form without the permission of the author. The views expressed in this book are not necessarily those of the publisher.

Due to the changing nature of the Internet, if there are any web addresses, links, or URLs included in this manuscript, these may have been altered and may no longer be accessible. The views and opinions shared in this book belong solely to the author and do not necessarily reflect those of the publisher. The publisher therefore disclaims responsibility for the views or opinions expressed within the work.

Unless otherwise indicated, Scripture quotations taken from the New King James Version (NKJV). Copyright © 1982 by Thomas Nelson, Inc. Used by permission. All rights reserved.

Paperback ISBN-13: 978-1-6628-3988-7
Ebook ISBN-13: 978-1-6628-3989-4

Table of Contents

Introduction ix
Chapter One—Character 1
Chapter Two—Perseverance.......................................41
Chapter Three—History Lessons 57
Chapter Four—Lessons From War 77
Chapter Five—Motivation 95
Chapter Six—The People Who Run Things 119
Chapter Seven—Gotta Love Your Family 129
Chapter Eight—The Church **153**
Chapter Nine—The Nature of God........................... 169
Chapter Ten—Lighter Moments.............................. 195

Endnotes... 235

Introduction

Author Ruth Rendell once said, "I get a lot of letters from people. They say: 'I want to be a writer. What should I do?' I tell them to stop writing to me and get on with it."[1] A track coach friend of mine told me, "Runners run." Well, I suppose it's also true that writers write. But I've spent over forty years teaching in private and public schools and preaching, and I "haven't had time to write." Oh, I've written a million words, but you know what I mean. I haven't written a book. Since I retired from teaching I now have no excuse for not getting the book done. What you have in your hands is the result.

In my defense, I *have* been a little busy. Teaching, preaching, and raising eleven kids (same wonderful wife, no adoptions, no twins) has been a bit time-consuming. Nevertheless, my adult children encouraged me several years ago to blog and share my thoughts on life, what I had learned, was learning, and hoped to learn from my experiences and the experiences of others, and I've been doing so. This book is a collection of some of those thoughts. I tried to keep in mind that people won't often tackle too much information at once, so the majority of the selections take only a few minutes to read. A few of them are condensed sermons and may run longer. One longer selection is about some of the funny things our kids said when they were growing up, and another is about our special needs daughter Laura, who has Down syndrome. Laura's story will bring you joy. Maybe someday I'll write a whole book about her life.

I pray that the reflections I've shared will be a blessing to you. I've not necessarily produced *profound* thoughts in these pages, but at least they are *my* thoughts, and posterity may one day be glad that I've put them down in writing. Perhaps they will be able to understand their father and grandfather better. I join that unknown author who once said, "One day I hope to write something of my own worth plagiarizing." My reflections express a biblical philosophy of life. I make no apologies for my Christian faith or worldview. Lincoln said the Bible is the best gift God ever gave to man[2], and for many reasons—this among them--he is my favorite president. Several of my blogs are meditations on his life. The best minds in history have thought deeply about the Bible's teachings and the meaning they have for their lives, so I'm in good company.

As I have grown older I have enjoyed learning lessons from reading history. I certainly hope that I have learned something from history besides learning nothing from history. What lessons there are for us in the exploits, the errors, and the stories of the past! We are inspired, warned, and guided by knowing what happened to others, and whether their responses were positive and healthy or negative and destructive.

Many of my stories are about my family and the church. They have been the central focus of my life, and the lessons I've learned there have been meaningful. I truly hope you enjoy the reflections. I consider my life a rich one, and I have always felt that we get more from life when we pause and reflect on it. One of my daughters gave me the idea to call my blog *The Quiet Corner*, and here are a few of the reflections from it. Many thanks to my parents who taught me, my wife who supports me, my children and grandchildren who continue to inspire me, and to everyone else, living or dead, that showed me something worthwhile to think about.

Bruce Howard
Hedley, Texas

Chapter One— Character

Dwight L. Moody once said, "Character is what you are in the dark."[3] God has promised to transform the character of those who love Him until it matches the character of the Lord Jesus. God uses many tools to build this character, and He demonstrates unwavering commitment to use whatever circumstances are necessary to form it. Abraham Lincoln said that character was like a tree, and reputation like a shadow. The shadow is what we think of it; the tree the real thing.[4] Let us grow in character as we journey through this life.

This chapter contains stories that highlight character—the character that some possess that is inspiring, and the flaws of some that remind us to improve our own character. Ultimately, character-building never ends until the day we meet our Lord and give account of our lives.

Adam and Eve Syndrome

I was ready to bolt out the door and travel to town when I noticed my left front tire was flat. I pumped it up so I could move the truck a bit, checked it out, and sure enough, there was a nail embedded in the tire. So I pumped it on up, drove it to the shop, and had them remove the nail and patch it up. As I paid out, the owner of the shop asked me, "Was this your fault or was it someone else's?" My reply was "As much as I'd like to blame this on somebody else, I'm about the only one who drives the truck, so I'll take responsibility for it."

How much like our ancestors Adam and Eve we are! It is hard-wired into our nature to want to blame someone else for our troubles. When confronted with his sin of eating the forbidden fruit, Adam immediately blamed Eve, and in a sense even cast blame on God Himself. Check out the actual answer from Genesis 3, but in our own words he was saying, "God, you gave me this woman, and look how she's brought me down. If she wasn't around I'd be fine." Then when God confronted Eve, she in essence said "It's not my fault; the devil made me do it." We see this knee-jerk reaction every time a politician gets caught in their hypocrisy. "It was a set-up," said Nancy Pelosi when she went to get her hair fixed at the salon she had closed down (without wearing a mask).[5] Politicians are very good at playing the "law is good for thee, but not for me" game. They want everyone else to follow the rules they spout, but they of course are exempt from those same rules because they are special. When caught red-handed, they say "I take full responsibility, but..." And you know that after the "but" they are going to disavow any responsibility and tell you how it's not their fault.

But before we get on our high horse and blast the politicians (surely the easiest of all targets), we ourselves find it easy to cast the blame somewhere else for messes that we create. It is vaguely possible that either my son or my wife were driving the truck when the nail entered the tire, but it is *very* likely that I'm the one who did it. So I am going to fight the urge to blame someone else, and I'll take responsibility without any buts. Lord, help me to conquer my penchant for playing the blame game. Most of the nails that slow me down in life are ones that I (and nobody else) ran over.

Don't Be Contrarian

A contrarian is one who does the opposite of public opinion, who goes against the flow. For some situations this is a dumb way to live. Society pushes back, hard, against those who stubbornly refuse to get on board with the consensus. For example, you may reasonably ask the question, "Why do Americans drive on the right side of the road?" (My own tongue-in-cheek answer is that we chose to do so because England drives on the left side of the road, and we long ago rebelled against their way of doing things). Anyway, it's not unreasonable to ask the question. What is unreasonable is to decide that you are going to do things differently here in America, do the opposite of public opinion and the laws of the road. "Nobody can push me around or tell me what to do. I'm going to drive on the left side of the road because I am my own person and march (or drive) to the beat of my own drum! Long live Britannia!" Go ahead, give it a try. Be contrarian.

But what will happen? The policeman won't let you continue to drive on the left side of the road. Why, because he's power-hungry? I doubt it. He understands that if you drive down the left side of the road somebody is going to get hurt. You are going to eventually have a big wreck, maybe a head-on collision, and it is going to destroy property and lives in a sad display of stupidity. It didn't have to happen, but you just wanted to be different and "do your own thing." If you persist in this behavior you will acquire many traffic violations, pay huge fines, and if persisted in long enough, you will find yourself in jail. Society is not going to let you continue to cause havoc and infringe upon the rights of others because you don't want to follow the rules everyone else follows.

Or you may be a student in class or a player on a team, and you decide to do things your own way. You might get away with a bit of this, but most teachers and coaches will put a stop to your going alone when it affects the good of everyone else. Good teaching and coaching don't usually involve chaos caused by everyone paddling the boat in different directions.

Many of the rules of society, some of them unwritten, are for our good. They bring order and sensibility to our lives. Imagine if every customer at the grocery store fought like a maniac to be first in the checkout line instead of waiting patiently for the people ahead of them to receive service (by the way, I've been to some third-world countries where fighting for the front is a normal way of life, and it's *not* a good custom—maybe there are some reasons it is still a third-world country). Rules bring clarity to what can be done and what can't be done, what should be done and what shouldn't be done.

So stop with the shortcuts, the gimmicks, the hare-brained stunts. Constantly paddling against the flow is an exhausting exercise, and gets you nowhere. Some people are contrarian just so they can say they are contrarian; but it is most often self-defeating. Sometimes it's just best to board your plane with group #8 like it says on your ticket instead of trying to cheat and sneak in with group #2.

When the risen Christ appeared to Paul on the road to Damascus, He asked Paul a pertinent question. "Why do you kick against the goads?" (Acts 26:14) In other words, "Why do you fight Me? My way is going to win out, and you are only hurting yourself by being in conflict with Me." The Lord has rules hard-wired into the fabric of the universe, and being contrarian to them is only going to result in your heartache and the heartache of those who love you.

"But wait!" you say. "Aren't there times we shouldn't be swayed by public opinion, times when it's good to live in a contrarian manner, to do things different from a lot of the herd?" That's a good point, and you can read all about it in the next blog. Maybe sometimes, in some ways, being a contrarian can be a good thing.

Be Contrarian

We explored how dumb it is to always be fighting societal rules, written or unwritten. It's not a good idea to drive on the wrong side of the road or go up the down escalator at the mall or be un-coachable just to prove you aren't an unthinking sheep who always does what it's told. Fair enough, but are there times it pays to go against the grain? Are there examples of behavior patterns that may be deemed unorthodox by the crowd but end up getting you to a better place in your life?

Obviously there are. An example might be in investing. What is the compulsive tendency of stock market investors when the prices of stocks start to rise? Well, that's when they want to get in, so they buy stocks as prices are going up. And what is the opposite tendency? To sell stocks when prices are dropping. But wait! When's the last time you went to the grocery store and bought all the items that were more expensive than normal and refused to buy any of the items when they were on sale? Being contrarian in your investing could mean just buying shares in your mutual fund every month regardless of the price of the shares. That way, when prices are lower because the market dips, you are getting things "on sale." It pays here *not* to follow the crowd, doesn't it?

Or if you are a student what about acting contrarian at times with regard to your schoolmates? Perhaps they have the typical attitude toward school, that the teacher is a doofus, that the assignments are dumb, that making good grades isn't that big of a deal, and "why do I need to know this stuff anyway?" A contrarian student here would realize that the teacher doesn't know everything, but they know more than the student; that maybe, just maybe, there *is* a reason to learn this stuff, and that one day having good grades might be very beneficial. So they do their best to learn what is presented. Or athletes who go contrarian and work like crazy to perfect their craft and really become *"all that they can be,"* in contrast to their teammates who coast along and try to get by with as little as possible. If you've seen the excellent movie *Greater* about the life and tragic death of Brandon Burlsworth you've seen a story about a contrarian athlete who worked extraordinarily hard to become an excellent football player. From flabby high school nerd to walk-on starter at the University of Arkansas to first-round draft pick of the Indianapolis Colts—an amazing story worth checking out.

And no matter how else you are contrarian, be contrarian with regard to our insane worldly culture. Jesus told His disciples that the world would hate them because it hated Him, and nothing has changed in 2000 years. If everyone in the world system agrees on something, a Christian can be pretty sure that it is wrong. Whatever the elites in

Hollywood and the media promote, you should question. Following Jesus means swimming upstream against popular culture. It means questioning the thinking behind the opinions and written or unwritten strictures imposed by our ruling class. It will mark you as contrarian perhaps, but in this case refusing to swallow worldly orthodoxy hook, line and sinker just makes you a smart fish.

Beef Masters

Not long ago I got to help John, a cattle breeder friend of mine, take a load of livestock to Montana. I had never really spent time in Big Sky country, and looked forward to the journey. We left early to outrun a late October snowstorm but weren't so successful, fighting deteriorating road conditions most of the way through Wyoming and southern Montana pulling a 32-foot trailer loaded with tons of livestock. We made it all in one piece and along the way I met some great folks, salt-of-the-earth types. I also learned quite a bit about the cattle industry. Since I barely knew which end of the beef to put the hay in, I had a lot to learn. The industry has moved a long way from "those two animals look pretty good; let's mate 'em up and see what we get."

John and his friends talked a lot about EPD's (expected progeny differences), RFI's (residual feed intakes) and other things with which I was unfamiliar. I met his friend Mark who works for a company that does genomic testing for a wide range of animals, including cattle. The breeders had sixteen traits that they tracked for the animals, including genes that affected tenderness of meat, docility in mothering, milk production, etc. They had spreadsheets on their animals that tracked birth weight, sell weight, pounds gained per day, food intake, and a host of other information. I discovered that despite the sometimes rough-cut exterior of these men and women, they were thoroughly sophisticated and extremely knowledgeable in a wide range of areas. It's a good thing I taught genetics for all those years! At least I wasn't totally at sea with their conversations. John told me that to be really successful in the business you had to be diligent to understand the traits you wanted in cattle, get them tested, and be careful in breeding.

Needless to say, I was impressed. It takes more than an inclination to spend time outdoors with animals to achieve success. It takes a detailed understanding of a plethora of issues, including animal health and psychology, herd behavior, genetics, entrepreneurial business models, and even human behavior if you want to make a profit as a breeder or commercial cattleman. And one more impressive thing about these folks; they have their heads set squarely on their shoulders. There is a strong moral fiber that runs through them, a virtue that makes them good folks to be around. I realized again that these are the kind of people that built the America we love. Too bad so few politicians ever really get to know citizens like these. They could learn a thing or two about hard work and integrity from them. Maybe those politicians should quit calling it "flyover" country, and fly in for a lesson or two about life from some of the greatest people on the planet.

Braunvieh cattle

Collections

Some people are collectors. I saw some interesting collections someone had compiled the other day. One man had over a thousand bowling balls stacked in a pyramid. Another had damaged golf balls he had found while he played different courses. One pediatrician collected all the strange things he found inside children's stomachs, including lots of coins, buttons, a guitar pick, a cross, and even a compass! Talk about a strange collection!

One man collected hundreds of keys and made a map of the United States with them. Another man loves Coca Cola and has kept every can since the time he was fifteen. He has tens of thousands of empty cans on display from all over the world...and a great big sugar high to go with it. Guys have lucky clover collections, medal collections, superhero collections, and shark tooth collections. There are funny eraser collections and old camera collections and old tool collections. There's even a woman who has collected all the crazy species of insects, spiders, and other odd animals from Australia and mounted them on her wall (yuck!).

What possesses folks to collect items? Probably lots of things: boredom; the desire to be unique and talked about; the beauty they find in some objects; the drive called Obsessive Compulsive Disorder. Who knows in some cases? But it is interesting and intriguing to many of us to watch as people spend countless hours and at times lots of money to find, collect, and display their treasures.

Now not to rain on anybody's parade, but maybe we ought to think about the fact that we only have one life to live, one chance to make an impact for the Lord while here on earth. Is it best when we spend inordinate amounts of time, energy, and resources on collecting stamps or spoons or coffee cups—or bowling balls, old cameras or shark teeth? Nothing immoral, illegal, or unethical about the habit of collecting, but what will happen to these collections once the collector passes on? Maybe an interested son or daughter will keep the collection or donate it to a museum someplace. They might want to remember their quirky parent by continuing to display the items. But most people—when it comes down to it—don't want hundreds of items cluttering up their homes, items like damaged golf balls or Coca Cola cans from around the world or odd items swallowed by children.

And worse than the fact that most of these collections may end up in the local dump is the fact that it is highly doubtful God will think the collection worth keeping. Each of these treasures painstakingly gathered will be part of those things burned up when the Lord destroys the earth with fire and rebuilds it anew. Jesus said don't collect treasures on earth, because they can rust or decay or be stolen. We are to instead store treasures in heaven where they can't be lost. (Matthew 6:19-20)

So maybe the collectors out there should collect some things that can't be taken away or destroyed. How about collecting good deeds (I Timothy 6:17) or memories of giving to others in their need (Luke 12:33) or ministering a cup of cold water to a thirsty child (Matthew 10:42)? How about collecting stories of sharing the gospel with those who have never heard or times of teaching Sunday school to children or teens or going on or supporting mission trips? Nothing wrong with collecting things; let's just make sure they are things that will never lose their value in light of eternity.

Country Folk

This summer I watched many of America's large liberal cities descending into anarchy, and it made me especially happy to be living in the rural part of the country. Even in the "big city" of Amarillo, Texas, where riots are more likely than out here in the sticks where I live, there was apparently fairly little unrest while Portland and Seattle burned. I saw a picture of an Amarillo police officer taking a selfie with a group of protesters and everyone seemed to be getting along.

Since I live here it is my biased view that the people of the panhandle of Texas are some of the best in the world. I know we have some crazies and malcontents, and there are still too many broken people who struggle to contribute to society in meaningful ways, but by and large most of the folks I know are hard-working, decent people who make good neighbors. I've never figured it was very mentally or emotionally healthy to crowd millions of bodies into small spaces. There is something extraordinarily soothing about driving past a herd of cattle in a field, or being away from the city where you can see a glorious Texas sunset or sunrise. And when you only have a few thousand people in your county, it makes you happier to see someone. If I lived in New York City (shudder), I think I would be constantly trying to avoid the large crowds instead of join them.

And add to these huge populations the liberal mayors and governors and city councils of large cities who promote liberal policies, you can see the resulting chaos and dysfunction. People there have been trained to expect the government to protect them, provide for them, and take care of their every need. Until people are expected to take care of themselves with God's help—until they learn to work hard, provide for their families, and stand on their own two feet—society won't work well. The people I know grew up learning to hoe cotton fields, plow and plant and harvest, build things, work cattle, do housework and repair the broken things around their homes and farms and ranches. In many cases they learned the adage "make do, or do without." They weren't *given* everything, but learned the joy of *earning* things with the sweat of their brow. No wonder they have character today. They don't have time to protest or riot. They're too busy providing for their families and contributing to society to tear it down.

I'm proud and happy to be among folks like this. My wife Gwynne and I just celebrated our fortieth wedding anniversary. You know you live in the country when you give your wife presents like a concrete floor for the garage, a trip to Amarillo for supper, a new hoe, and two new watering cans for her garden. And she loves them! It's nice to be country folk. We don't loot our stores and burn down our police stations.

God's Fiduciary

I was in a bank the other day and noticed the word fiduciary. It's a funny-sounding word to people who don't work in financial institutions, certainly not a word we use every day in normal life. I've never been in a conversation with my friends or family and used the word, and if I did, I'm sure they would all give me a quizzical look.

It's not only an interesting term, it also relates to a meaningful principal for the Christian faith. The word fiduciary is a financial and legal term that comes from the Latin *"fiducia"* which means trust. To have a fiduciary relationship is for one side to trust the other to handle its affairs. If you deposit your money in a savings account at the bank, for example, you have made them a fiduciary of your money. You assume you can go back to the bank and withdraw some of the money you have entrusted with them. When a person puts money in an investment firm that person trusts the managers of the account to act in their best interest, to increase the value of their holdings. When you have a fiduciary relationship with another you expect to be able to hold them accountable; that they will deal with your resources in a way that meets with your approval. If you want money out of your mutual fund account, you expect to be able to pick up the phone or use the computer to indicate your desire, and the managers of that account will sell some shares and send the money to you. For them to keep the money or use it to their own advantage without consulting you is called fraud, and you would rightly be angered if they did such a thing. They stole some of your resources for their own gain.

God has a fiduciary relationship with believers, whether they know it or not. He has loaned us many resources during our years on earth, resources that ultimately belong solely to Him. He has granted us the use of time, energy, health, money, talents, and relationships, and He trusts us to manage these resources at His direction. For us to ignore His wishes, or to abuse the resources He loans us, or to use these resources solely for our own pleasure and comfort without regard to

His directions on how they should be used, is for us to defraud Him. The Bible tells us we are stewards for God, that we cannot assume the resources are our own, that every good and perfect gift comes down from the Father of lights (James 1:17), and the Father has specific uses for all those resources. We should manage them for His glory at all times.

It is a high calling to be God's fiduciary. You have been given many things He wants you to use under His direction. You are to "invest" everything in ways that makes them grow, and then use those resources to bring about the increase of His kingdom. Be a trustworthy fiduciary. You don't want to stand before God at the end of your life and try to explain why you failed Him, when He trusted you to manage His affairs.

How Do You Get There?

When I taught school I loved the phrase *"It isn't rocket science!"* I loved it first of all because it's true; success in life isn't that complicated. Students at times would say to me, *"This stuff (Chemistry or Physics) is too hard."* Well, how does it become a lot easier?
1) Come EARLY—get help
2) Stay LATE—get help
3) PRACTICE on your own—then get FEEDBACK and help
4) Schedule time in your day to practice, and if you need it GET HELP

It's not rocket science! The reason things remain hard for most of us is that we are *unwilling* to do the simple things required for them to become easier for us. It's not the *material* that is too hard, it's the *discipline* to learn the material that is hard.

Jonas Salk, the man who came up with the vaccine for polio, was famous for reminding us, "The only place success comes before work is in the dictionary."[6] That goes for pretty much everything. If you think you are going to ease your way into accomplishing something grand, something worth having, you are delusional. All worthwhile things come because we pushed through, learned the hard lessons, and fought our way through the obstacles to find the solutions we needed. *That's how you "get there", wherever it is you want to go.* Josh Billings once said "Consider the postage stamp: its usefulness consists in the ability to stick to one thing until it gets there."[7] Be like the postage stamp, and stick with it until you are where you want to be.

By the way, the second reason I loved the phrase "It isn't rocket science…"? When I taught physics we had a unit on planets and orbits, and I could tell the students, *"You're finally about to learn some rocket science!!"*

How to Waste Millions

> Everyone thinks that if they win the lottery they'll be set, but you may be old enough or wise enough (hopefully both) to know better. It's always good to be reminded that lots of money doesn't make up for stupid.[8]
>
> *When he signed his pro football contract with a Canadian team it was the highest contract ever. His estimated lifetime earnings are over 20 million dollars. ***Rocket Ismail***
>
> *Four-time heavyweight champion of the world with an estimated lifetime income of 250 million dollars. ***Evander Holyfield***
>
> *Considered one of the greatest defensive players in the history of football, this hall-of-famer won two Super Bowls with the New York Giants. His estimated lifetime income was 50 million dollars. ***Lawrence Taylor***
>
> *The youngest man ever to win the WBC, WBA, and IBC world heavyweight titles. Estimated income of 300-400 million dollars. ***Mike Tyson***

*One of basketball's 50 all-time greatest players, 6-time NBA champion who played for the Chicago Bulls with Michael Jordan. Estimated income 120 million dollars. ***Scottie Pippen***

*One of baseball's sweetest swings, this left-hander played many years in the majors and had a net income exceeding 20 million dollars. ***Jack Clark***

*At the time of her retirement considered the greatest woman basketball player of all time, she won three Olympic gold medals and was a 3-time WNBA Player of the Year. Estimated income 50 million dollars. ***Cheryl Swoopes***

And we could go on...and on...and on. But we won't. You know what happened. Bad business decisions, terrible investments, illegal behavior that netted prison time, expensive hobbies (one owned 18 cars, one costing over $700,000, and another likes buying private jets), out-of-wedlock children needing child support, lawsuits, drugs, tax evasion, you name it—every dumb decision in the book.

Virtually all of them have bills they can't pay; most declared bankruptcy along the way. Proverbs 16:16 says, "How much better to get wisdom than gold, to get insight rather than silver." A lot of people can make money, but only the wise know how to spend it wisely, give generously, and keep some of it for a rainy day. We need lots of wisdom far more than lots of money.

It Won't Kill You

I had the privilege of sitting on a committee to choose a regional employee of the year, and it was very interesting. The four finalists—although unique in their own right—shared one crucial character trait: they were all hard workers. We had an hour with each candidate, and it was obvious that they did their jobs with energy and zeal. They were willing to roll up their sleeves and join their communities in making them better. Each had intelligence and vision, but none claimed to be the brightest bulb in the chandelier. Their success was a result of diligently working to improve themselves and their organizations.

My brother is an athletic director, and he told me a story about a young man who came into their coaching ranks who knew nothing about coaching, but who had a strong work ethic. He said within a few months this young man had become a good coach, and that he would become a great coach within a few years. Why? Was it the stellar resume he brought to the job? No, the young man had never coached before. It was the young man's willingness to take on any task, no matter how menial, and give his best to seeing the task done well. Unfortunately in our society that trait is in relatively short supply.

But many of the people I know understand the value of hard work. One of our church members is a 98-year-old WWII veteran. There aren't many of those guys left anymore, but hopefully you know one too. He grew up hard scrabble and made hard work an eleventh commandment: "Thou shalt work from dawn to dusk every day and take care of business without complaining." He never expected anybody to give him anything, but believed that if he wanted something he could go out and fetch it if he worked hard enough. His son-in-law said that when the old man was in his seventies you could hardly keep up with him, and the son-in-law was in his forties at the time. This old man is the kind of guy that builds communities and churches, a man who just a couple of years ago was up on a ladder nailing down some metal on his shed. When the son-in-law got onto him, his response was classic, "Well, it's not going to get done by itself." So at 96 he was making sure it got done.

And then there's a twelve-year-old boy who lives down the street. His sister told me the other day he was out in the community offering to mow lawns for folks, and in the brief time out of school for summer vacation he had already made $200. Later that day when I saw the young man I shook his hand and congratulated him on his initiative and willingness to work for what he wanted.

We really should never be surprised when people are successful. The principles to achieving it are universal and work for every generation...

*In all labor there is profit—Proverbs 14:23

*Whoever works his land will have plenty of bread—Proverbs 12:11

*The hand of the diligent will rule—Proverbs 12:24

*Whoever is slack in his work is a brother to him who destroys—Proverbs 18:9

*A slack hand causes poverty, but the hand of the diligent is rich—Proverbs 10:4

*The plans of the diligent lead surely to abundance—Proverbs 21:5

And we could go on, but you get the drift. Not only will hard work not kill you, but hard work is the universal ticket to getting the most out of life, especially when you follow the advice of the apostle Paul in Colossians 3:23 "And whatever you do, do it heartily, as to the Lord rather than men..."

Keep Alert

You know the old adage about assuming things. Well, we sometimes assume that people know what they are doing. Most of the time our assumptions are justified, but sometimes it doesn't pay to trust another to get it right. When considering children and chores we must *expect* but also *inspect* to make sure the task is completed properly.

I know someone who trusted a financial broker to take care of her affairs. Turns out the broker charged over $28,000 for a year's work, and the investments far underperformed mutual funds that were passively managed. Needless to say, when the "oops" was discovered the broker was fired, because, as some have quipped, he was a financial advisor making his client broker and broker and broker.

I had a situation once where some work was done on my house, and not being an expert at plumbing or anything else to do with construction, I left it up to the expert to do the job. Except about the time he was finished and I paid him, I discovered the job wasn't done right at all, and I (with the help of my father) got to learn how to fix the plumbing myself anyway. I would love to blame the workman, but it was my fault for not inspecting it along the way.

God has given you the great privilege of running your own life. You can't give it over to someone else and expect them to be diligent while you nap. They are responsible for themselves, and you are responsible for you. Don't fall asleep."Be sober, be vigilant; because your adversary the devil walks about like a roaring lion, seeking whom he may devour." (I Peter 5:8) You can't blame someone else if he takes a bite out of you because you were too lazy to pay attention.

Quit Pouring the Quicksand

I heard a story about dealing with temptation the other day that caught my attention. A pastor told the story of a man in his church who committed adultery with a young woman at the office. When the man confessed the sin to his wife, their marriage hit the rocks. Now he was in for counseling, and the pastor asked him, "So explain to me how this happened?"

"Well, pastor, the temptation was just too overwhelming, and I found I couldn't help myself." "Okay, how did you meet Jenny (the woman with whom he had the affair)?"

"Well, I met her a year ago when she started working for our office, and I thought, 'Wow, she's good-looking.'"

"Okay, so what happened then?"

"I started walking by her desk on purpose so I could have a short discussion with her about jobs we were doing."

"Okay, what happened then?"

"When I was instructed to put a team together to work on a project, I made sure that Jenny was selected to help."

"What happened after that?"

"We were supposed to go work on a big project in Vegas, so I asked Jenny to go along to help with it."

"And then…?"

"Well, after a long, hard day's work the group was going to go out for some food and drinks and I asked Jenny to join us."

"Then what?"

"After we returned to the motel I walked Jenny to her room, and, you know, things just got out of control."

At that point the pastor said this to the man, "You told me the temptation was just too great, and that you couldn't overcome it. Man, you ended up in quicksand that you poured yourself!" And how true it is. This man's life had fallen apart, his family was now in shambles, his reputation as a believer now a byword to others, and he was in misery, bowing under the weight of guilt because he *was* guilty. But it wasn't because he suddenly ran into some overwhelming temptation. He had worked pretty hard to set up the situation where the temptation was overwhelming. He had poured his own quicksand, and then seemed surprised that it dragged him under.

I Corinthians 10:13 is clear, "No temptation has overtaken you except such as is common to man; *but God is faithful, who will not allow you to be tempted beyond what you are able,* but with the temptation will also make the way of escape, that you may be able to bear it." (emphasis mine) So let's not hear any more of this nonsense about the temptation just being too overwhelming to fight. Instead, let's remember that it was this man's own fault that he fell, because he spent a year or more pouring his own quicksand. And let's also remember not to pour any of our own.

Resigned Thinking

If you ask little children what they want to do when they grow up, they'll give you fantastic goals…be a doctor, play pro ball, be a ballerina, become a millionaire. When you ask teenagers the same question, they often give much less idealistic answers, and part of that is good. I'm not playing pro ball if I'm 5'9" tall, weigh 140 pounds, run a five-second 40-yard dash, and bench press 200 pounds. Neither does everyone have the brains, the determination, and the background to be a neurosurgeon. But a main reason we lower our goals is *failure*.

People engage in resigned thinking because they've failed. They've tried things and didn't do so hot, so they gave up. I was an "A" student in school when I took my first chemistry course, but my average for that course was a "C". If you had asked me then whether I would like to make a career teaching chemistry, I would have seriously thought you were nuts. I *hated* chemistry! It made me feel like a failure.

But while getting a degree in Biology Education I needed to take some chemistry courses, and I survived them. Still, after college graduation, I would never have dreamed of teaching chemistry. Maybe I didn't hate it, but let's just say it wasn't on my favorite-things-to-do list.

Fast forward to my becoming a teacher at Lake Country Christian School. I was the only science teacher in the high school at the time, we had sophomores in our school, and it was time to teach chemistry. I looked for help, but nobody else knew anything about the subject. I *had* to learn it so I could teach it. I went to the local university bookstore, bought a college chemistry book, and began to study.

And I ended up teaching it for 38 years. It became far and away my favorite subject to teach.

Remember that real failure is simply giving up too soon or never trying. Thomas Edison once said, "I haven't failed; I've just found

10,000 ways that won't work."⁹ If you had given in to resigned thinking you never would have walked, never would have learned to ride a bike or drive a car, never asked that girl to marry you, and never tried being a parent. Don't give in to it today either. You have a challenging situation? Good, it's something to overcome with God's help. Let your character grow as you conquer it. No more resigned thinking.

The Favor of God

Every person wants to walk in the favor of God, but this does *not* mean...

1) GOD PLAYS FAVORITES. The Bible teaches a person's status or wealth or talent or piety do not make them one that God will favor over another. God used a huge variety of people to glorify His name in Scripture: poor shepherds, maidens, carpenters, fishermen, farmers, and foreigners. He also used those in positions of wealth and power: people like Job and Joseph and Daniel and Isaiah and Esther. He used religious leaders and He used Mary Magdalene. God favors many different kinds of people.

2) THINGS WILL ALWAYS GO WELL. Noah found grace in the eyes of the Lord, but he was mocked by his generation. Joseph walked in the favor of God but was unjustly thrown into the pit and prison. Moses was the friend of God but suffered. Ruth certainly had no easy time of it, and Esther didn't either. Daniel was favored of God but had a very difficult life in many ways. And Mary, who was *highly* favored, was misunderstood by Joseph, had a traumatic birthing experience, was lonely when Joseph died and Christ left home to begin His ministry, and was in anguish as she watched her Son cruelly crucified before her eyes. Knowing the favor of God certainly doesn't mean experiencing easy street.

3) WE CAN DEMAND OR EARN HIS FAVOR. We are saved by grace, and it is by grace alone through faith alone that we can walk with God. God does not operate a meritocracy, where we earn credits by doing well and get demerits for bad behavior. Though God freely gives favor, He will never be bullied into owing us favor. Scripture is equally clear on that score.
4) YOU CAN ALWAYS TELL ON THE SURFACE WHICH PERSON IS FAVORED. Humans are apt to point to convenient circumstances or wealth or success and assume the person on top has the favor of God, while the person on the bottom is cursed of God. Scripture references will show this is not always true. Psalm 37 tells us about the wicked that prosper, and says they will eventually pay for their wickedness despite their relative success on earth. They certainly don't have God's favor. Job walked in the favor of God until…the bottom dropped out of his life. And at the end he again was favored. But in a real sense he was favored by God right in the middle of his trauma, for the story of Job, one of the oldest in the Bible, has blessed and instructed hundreds of millions of people, and given them courage to trust God in the midst of their own agonies. What about the rich man and Lazarus? The one on top seemed to enjoy God's blessings, while the one on bottom seemed to be cursed. But how did that story pan out for the men in it? And the Lord Jesus Himself went to the cross, not as a punishment for His own misdeeds or wandering from God, but rather as sign of God showing favor to us who did not deserve it.

With those things favor does *not* mean, Scripture also tells us God is willing to show His favor to those He loves, and that we can experience and *expect* His favor…

1) Moses expected it. In Psalm 90 he says "satisfy us early with Your mercy (favor)" and "make us glad (favored)" and "let the beauty (favor) of the Lord our God be upon us."

2) David expected it. In several psalms he says God delights in him...
   a) Psalm 5:12—"For You, O Lord, will bless the righteous; with *favor* You will surround him as with a shield."
   b) Psalm 30:5—His anger is but for a moment, His favor is for life...
3) Other psalmists expected it. Psalm 67:1—"God be merciful to us and bless us (speak well of us, grant us favor), and cause His face to shine upon us. Psalm 84 says, "I will sing of the mercies (favors) of the Lord forever..."
4) Solomon expected it. Proverbs 3:3-4—"let not mercy and truth forsake you; bind them around your neck, write them on the tablet of your heart, and so find favor and high esteem in the sight of God and man." Proverbs 3:34 says, "The curse of the Lord is on the house of the wicked, but He blesses (favors) the home of the just, surely He scorns the scornful, but gives grace (favor) to the humble."
5) Isaiah expected it. Isaiah 58:11—"The Lord will guide you continually, and satisfy your soul in drought, and strengthen your bones; you shall be like a watered garden, and like a spring of water whose waters do not fail." If this is not a description of God's favor I don't know what is.

Why would God show favor and how can we experience this favor? The answer to the first question is found in the character of God. Why does God give grace? He is gracious. Why does He bless? He is a blesser. Why does He show favor? It is His *pleasure*. Psalm 37:23 says the steps of a good man are ordered by the Lord and that God *delights* in his (the man's) way. Favor is how God demonstrates His delight. God shows His approval in a *tangible* way. You give money at God's directive, and He blesses you with more so you can give more. You trust God has sent you on a mission trip, and you see His favorable hand in getting through customs, reaching people with the gospel, helping get the church planted, and helping you come home safely. In Luke 12:32

Jesus said it is God's pleasure to give us the kingdom. God likes handing out favors to His flock.

The 2nd question is also easy to verify by the plumb line of scripture. If the question is "can we do anything to *earn* God's favor?" the answer is no. If the question is "can we do something to *experience* more of God's favor in our lives?" the answer is an unqualified YES!

1) Psalm 1 says the man is favored who does not walk in the counsel of the ungodly but whose delight is in the law of the Lord. God delights in and favors those who *delight in Him.* The steps of a *good man* are ordered by the Lord; the man seeking God, committed to following God's ways, a man who delights in God Himself. This is David's point because a few verses before this is one of the all-time favorite verses in the Psalms: "Delight yourself in the Lord and He shall give you the desires of your heart." (Psalm 37:4) When you delight in God He delights in favoring you.

2) We see the favor of God when we are *humble.* Solomon said the favor of God is on the humble, and it so impressed Peter and James that they both put it into their epistles. God shows grace (favor) to the humble. Isaiah 66:2 says the same thing, "These are ones I look on with favor; those who are humble and contrite of spirit…"

3) Ephesians 2:8-9 says we are saved by grace through faith. Hebrews 11:6 says without faith it is impossible to please God. God is favorable to *believers.* Faith pleases God. Stepping out in faith is required to walk with God. God delights in pouring His favor on those whose obedience compels them to risk something for God and His kingdom.

4) God favors those who are His *friends.* 2nd Chronicles 16:9 says, "For the eyes of the Lord run to and fro throughout the whole earth, to show Himself strong on behalf of them whose heart is perfect toward him." To be "perfect" toward Him means we seek His favor more than we seek the favor of anyone else, even ourselves. God favors those who love Him and His commandments. If someone in our church needed help, we would gladly help them. We might

not be so quick to help someone we don't know well. The difference between the two is that one is part of our church *family*, and among our dearest *friends*. You could say that we favor our friends over strangers. God does too.

5) The favor of God is a sense that God is on our side, fighting for us, providing and caring for us regardless of circumstances. To experience God's favor is to be *content* with Him alone. So Paul and Silas felt favored of God even though beaten and thrown into prison. Peter and John felt favored of God when they were arrested, beaten and reprimanded, "rejoicing that they were counted worthy to suffer shame for His name." (Acts 5:41) The favor of God involves His direction in our lives. All those who were favored of God in the Bible knew God was with them, discovered their role in the great drama of redemption, and walked confidently toward fulfilling that goal, despite hardships, obstacles, enemies, and death. The worst thing in life is not to have hard things happen to you, or resistance from your culture, or to suffer, but to have lived your life climbing the ladder leaning against the wrong building. You may make it to the top, but every step you took was going the wrong way.

I pray that you walk in the favor of God today. It is His pleasure to give it to those who love Him.

The Green-Eyed Monster

Most of us know the first of the Ten Commandments: have no other gods before Me. (Exodus 20) How many of us know the last one? In simple terms it is don't covet, or don't envy what others have. In primitive cultures there is often a problem with understanding ownership. The thought is "If you have something, then I have something. When your back is turned I'm going to take what I want from you." Foreigners from more civilized countries are routinely flummoxed by this attitude, and see the primitives as irredeemable thieves.

In countries governed by law, we have taken a more biblical approach to ownership. When a person has a home or land or stuff that they have legally purchased, we rightly understand that the things belong to them, and that for us to try and take them is a form of thievery, which goes back to commandment #8. God says don't do it.

But commandment #10 goes further. God desires us to understand that if we want something we should go out and earn it, apply ourselves honestly to the hard work necessary to gain ownership of the thing. If someone does this and can afford a nice car or home or boat, more power to them. It's never our place to gaze with longing on their things and want them for ourselves if we are not willing to put out the effort it takes to acquire those things.

You want the kind of things the doctor has? Go to the trouble of spending half your life in school and sacrificing like he did. Wish you had a nice retirement nest egg? Apply yourself to working for a company that provides nice benefits, and invest your money wisely over a long period of time. That money doesn't get there by accident. You want to win with money? Quit playing the lottery, getting into excessive debt, and foolishly spending what money you do have. Read some good books on money management, and apply the suggestions.

It is easy to be jealous. We look at what another has and wish we could have that too. Well, in the first place, some things aren't worth having. You admire the house, the cars, and the boat, but don't understand that the person is in debt up to their eyeballs to have all those things. Or perhaps they do have lots of money, but money, if not managed God's way, can quickly become a curse, as many rich folks have discovered. Finally, learn true contentment. There is nothing wrong with wanting a better car, as long as you are willing to work hard enough to afford it. But there's also nothing wrong with being happy with your old car, if it runs okay. Contentment doesn't mean we don't desire some things, but it does mean we have made the decision to be happy with what we have if we can't get those things. Paul would agree. "Now godliness with contentment is great gain." (I Timothy 6:6) Kill the green-eyed monster of jealousy. Be happy for your neighbor, and for what God has given you.

The Standing Frame

When our daughter Laura was little she became an expert in the "scoot across the floor on your bottom" style of moving about the room. Because of her Down syndrome she had weak legs, and so she didn't want to walk or even stand up very long. The physical therapist who worked with her during those days provided for us a "standing frame", a device that makes an infant stand up and put pressure on their legs to strengthen them. Boy, did Laura hate that thing! She would cry and wail every time we put her in it, and even though it began as only a ten-minute exercise, you'd have thought we were torturing her for hours by the agonized screams she uttered. She would begin crying at the sight of it.

But it worked. As we slowly increased her time in the frame, her legs got stronger, and eventually she could stand on her own two feet, and walk. What a lesson for us all! How often in life we complain about a problem or hardship, and we moan and groan because we have to push back against it. But the very hardship is a means for us to have to stand on our own two feet, and if we don't learn to carry our own weight, how will we ever grow up to carry the weight of others who depend on us; our spouses and children and members of the larger community?

Galatians 6 has one of those conundrums that are fairly common in scripture. Verse 2 says we are to "bear one another's burdens, and so fulfill the law of Christ." Then verse 5 says "For each one shall bear his own load." Wait a minute. If each person bears their own load then we shouldn't have to help them bear it, right? But obviously not everyone bears their own load, and in a sense probably none of us completely bears our own load at all times. We are all subject to times of illness or discouragement or spiritual weakness where we find ourselves struggling to carry our own burdens, and the thought of helping someone else carry theirs is a bridge too far.

So we all need help at times carrying burdens, and often the Lord uses others to help us carry ours, and we should be available to help them carry theirs. But we all know people in our culture that don't seem able to ever carry theirs. They were never able to train themselves to stand on their own two feet and carry their own weight. And sadly, nobody made them get in the standing frame. Think of the standing frames God put in your life as you learned to carry yourself and be responsible; learned to get yourself out of bed, go to work, earn a living, and pay your bills. You might have screamed bloody murder while you endured them, but they gave you the strength to not only care for yourself, but to become a burden-bearer for others, and thus fulfill the law of Christ.

The Two Sides of Blessing

A friend was telling me the other day of a tremendous financial blessing he had received from the Lord, and followed with the comment, "We are now making decisions about how we can bless others." It was a reminder that every blessing— which by definition is something that makes us happy, excited, good news, something that benefits us— brings with it a responsibility.

We are blessed with a wonderful spouse—so we in turn must be the best spouse we can be. We are blessed with a child (or children)—so we in turn must raise them in the nurture and admonition of the Lord. We are blessed with a financial windfall or the meeting of a financial need— so we in turn must use our resources to bless others with our tithes and gifts. We are blessed with physical health or a healing of disease or injury—so we in turn must use our bodies ever more to help others and fulfill our duties.

There is no blessing without a following responsibility to in turn bless others. As the old hymn goes, "Count your blessings, name them one by one..." And then figure out how God wants you to be responsible with each blessing in turn. Both Paul and Peter told us to use the gifts we've been given to bless and serve others (Romans 12:6 and I Peter 4:10).

Lord, send me a blessing today, and then as another old hymn says, *"Make me a blessing..."* Never forget the other side of the blessing coin.

Two Sets of Threes

Hugh, a Depression-era Indiana farmer, was struggling to make ends meet as it was. But then disaster struck. He had borrowed money to buy thirty hogs, which he intended to raise, breed, and sell for profit. He put up his house and farm as collateral for the loan. Needing to inoculate the hogs against cholera, he purchased the vaccine and gave them the shots. The vaccine was defective, and all thirty hogs died. At the same time a drought came that killed off most of the wheat, corn, and alfalfa they grew to sell. Hugh's sole means of supporting the family was now gone, and the bank foreclosed on the farm.

But out of this terrible hard time came a lesson one of Hugh's sons would never forget. Hugh was a faithful Christian, a daddy who read the Scripture every night to his children. He was fond of sayings that he wanted to pass down to others, a trait his son would make a central part of his life and career. One of Hugh's sayings for his sons was "Two Sets of Threes": ***Never lie, never cheat, never steal; don't whine, don't complain, don't make excuses.*** Now here was a chance for Hugh to demonstrate to his family that he really believed what he said. His son would later write of this time, "Through it all, Dad never winced. He laid no blame on the merchant who had sold him the bad serum, didn't curse the weather, and had no hatred toward the banker. As instructive as it was to hear him recite the two sets of threes, seeing him abide by them as he lost the farm had a powerful effect on me. That's where I came to see that what you do is more important than what you say you'll do." [10]

Boy, how easy is it to talk a big game! We sometimes think that it is as easy to walk the talk as it is to talk the talk, but then we are confronted with reality and find out just how difficult it is to live by our own convictions. Convictions aren't really convictions if they disappear when it gets hard. I am struck by how many of the psalms deal with the difficulty of actually trusting God when things fall apart. Many times the psalmist cries out to God in despair, in heartache, and in agony of soul, wondering at times if God hears or cares, only to resolve the issue at the end and record that God will come through, even in times of desperation. Psalm 22, a psalm of David, is just one example; one with a message powerful enough for Christ to quote from the cross. It begins "My God, My God, why have You forsaken Me? Why are You so far from helping me, and from the words of my groaning?" Yet after being "poured out like water," with a heart "like wax," and with strength "dried up like a potsherd," brought "to the dust of death," the psalmist concludes that "my praise shall be of You (God) in the great assembly; I will pay my vows before those who fear Him...Those who seek Him will praise the Lord."

Trusting God is easy when life is easy. Walking with God through the valley is where you find out how much you really trust Him. But if you will trust Him in the valley, your children will find your life lessons ones they will never forget. Oh, speaking of the impact of a life lesson, who was the son, the one who never forgot the integrity of Hugh's life? Only the greatest men's college basketball coach of all time: John Wooden. Wooden won an incredible ten national championships, including seven in a row at one point. No men's college coach in history has come close to that record. His was a life of integrity, like his father, who John saw live out what he taught.

Wait!

You'd think it's the easy thing to do. You don't have to do anything except go on with your life. It requires no action on your part other than what you know you are to keep on doing. Why is it so hard?

Somehow we think we must be in *control*. Why did Adam and Eve eat the fruit? Why did Cain kill Abel? Why did Saul sacrifice animals for victory when he knew God had not sanctioned it? They grew tired of waiting for God to move, so they took things into their own hands. They wanted to make the decisions, even if they are wrong. It's why scripture tells us more than one hundred times to wait on Him...

1) Isaiah 40:31—They that wait upon the Lord shall renew their strength, mount up with wings as eagles, run and not be weary, walk and not faint. *We will faint if we don't wait.*
2) Psalm 27:13-14—"I would have lost heart, unless I had believed that I would see the goodness of the Lord in the land of the living. Wait on the Lord. Be of good courage..." *Without waiting we lose heart and our courage fails.*
3) Lamentations 3:25—"The Lord is good to those who wait for Him, to the soul who seeks Him." *Waiting is a way for our souls to seek Him and experience His goodness.*
4) Proverbs 3:5-6—"Trust in the Lord with all your heart and lean not on your own understanding. I all your ways acknowledge Him... *To acknowledge means to accept, allow, admit, concede, confess, realize, recognize, and appreciate.*[11] *All these involve a form of waiting. And it is then that God directs your path.*
5) James 5:7-8—"Therefore be patient, brethren, until the coming of the Lord. See how the farmer waits for the precious fruit of the earth, waiting patiently for it until it receives the early and latter rain. You also be patient..." *Anticipate harvest; it is a blessed thing when it finally comes. As the plants grow, so we grow.*
6) 2nd Peter 3:9—"The Lord is not slack concerning His promise... not willing that any should perish but that all should come to repentance..." *One reason God doesn't bring the curtain down on humanity is His mercy for those who will repent. Wait for His judgment; it will come in due time.*
7) Psalm 33:20-21—"Our soul waits for the Lord; He is our help and our shield. For our heart shall rejoice in Him. *Waiting gives us a special fellowship with others who wait.*

Chapter One—Character

There are many benefits to waiting on the Lord. He is not holding out on us, but His intent is to bless us with every good and perfect gift as we wait on Him. But as you'll see in the next reflection, waiting is not passive.

Wait While You Walk

I'm going on a big hike in October, so I've been told to get in shape for it. To do so I am walking several times a week. I can't run any more, it's too hard on my knees, but the walking is good exercise in every way. I've moved up from about three miles to six miles each time I walk. It sure is the slow way to see the world. The roads I walk are pretty lonely; I only see a few cars in over an hour and a half. Nevertheless, when a vehicle does pass me I am very aware of our relative speeds. What will take me over an hour and forty-five minutes takes them a bit over five minutes to traverse.

As I was walking the other day I was reminded of Isaiah 40:31, a pretty famous passage. "They that wait upon the Lord shall renew their strength; they shall mount up with wings as eagles. They shall run and not be weary; they shall walk and not faint." I have heard some say that this describes the relative strength God gives us in our stages of life; that God helps us soar when we are young, run during middle age, and continue to walk and press on as we get older. That sounds plausible to me. Be that as it may, there is a conundrum within the verse. How do we get the strength to soar, run, and walk? By *waiting*. But waiting seems a verb of *inaction*, while soaring, running, and walking are definitely *action* words. How can inaction give strength for action?

Undoubtedly there are several connections. To wait could mean to rest, and surely we must rest in between our periods of action. If not for rest, eventually we would collapse. God has built into the fabric of our humanity a need for pause, for refreshing, for renewal. This is true *daily* (hence our need for sleep), but also *weekly* (hence the Sabbath). The cycle of action followed by inaction breaks down when we don't stop to recharge the batteries.

It is also plausible, and probable, that waiting on the Lord occurs not in between our acts of service to Him and others, but *during* those acts. In other words, we have a need, perhaps something about which it seems we can do nothing. We cannot get that new job, change the heart of that child or boss or loved one, decide which door to walk through, or whether to stay put where we are and not walk through any of them. Do we always put our lives on hold during these times? Of course not! We give the Lord the situation, then we get up and go to school, go to work, go about our regular activities. The truth is that we walk *while* we wait. And God in His time will either give us that new job or give us contentment in our old job; God will bring that loved one back to Himself; God will give us peace to choose which door to go through or to stay exactly where we are.

Waiting on the Lord is biblical; it is mentioned many times in scripture, especially in the Psalms. And there may be times we actually stop, rest, and wait for God to act. But it is also likely that we will need to keep walking while we wait. And as we walk, or run, or fly, God will give us strength to carry on until He does what only He can do. Unless God directs, don't let your waiting keep you from doing the work you know you've been called to do.

What Price Fame?

We are very aware that some people are totally insane. The BBC recently reported on gym trainer T Siva following a disturbing trend among young adults of taking selfies as close to moving trains as possible.[12] You might check out the viral video of Mr. Silva standing near the tracks in Hyderabad, India, filming himself as he is hit by the transport train. He ignored warnings from both the blaring horn of the conductor and from a person nearby who told him he was too close to the juggernaut. This daring game has caught on, especially in India. In October

2017 three teenagers were run over by a train while trying to take a selfie in Karnataka State, and two teenagers were killed while taking selfies on railway tracks in Delhi.

Many who have watched this trend and the video of Mr. Siva being hit by the train call it "shocking". But isn't that sometimes the point of selfies? Everybody wants to be "famous" for something, wants to be recognized by others as having courage to do what others dare not do. It's what causes people every year to fall off the rim of the Grand Canyon while someone takes their picture. "Hey, take a picture of me while I say 'oops, I slipped.'" (We should have asked when we had the chance what they wanted us to sing at their funeral). What is the price of such self-absorbed behavior? Grieving relatives and friends, angry community administrators and leaders, and obviously narrow escapes, serious injuries or even death for the perpetrators. And did these folks taking selfies think about the train engineer? They say that engineers are instructed to shut their eyes or turn away when they realize they are going to run over someone on the tracks. The memories and feelings of that traumatic event haunt many railroad operators for the rest of their lives.

The apostle Paul reminds us in Ephesians 5:15-17 that we should walk circumspectly (unwilling to take unnecessary and foolish risks) and wisely, and to "redeem the time", understanding the will of God. So how about young people in India and elsewhere getting involved helping an elderly person or cleaning their city instead of foolishly exposing themselves to harm in order to impress their "friends" on Facebook? It certainly would not be God's will for you to stand on a railroad track and hope you didn't get hit. That might fall under the category of "tempting the Lord your God." You might go down in history with your fifteen minutes of fame, but only as a byword as another fool who wasted their lives pursuing frivolous things.

What We Learn From Labor

"In all labor there is profit." (Proverbs 14:23) Labor is defined as mental or physical work, especially difficult or fatiguing mental or physical work. [13] Labor doesn't sound like a fun word, but this proverb says it is always profitable. What do we learn from labor?

1) We realize we can work **LONGER** than we thought we could. This builds *endurance*, and Scripture is big on endurance. Old-timers talk about working "can to can't"—from the time in the morning you can first see until the time at night that you can't see. Sometimes it takes long hours to accomplish what needs to be done. Blessed are those who endure to get the job finished.

2) We realize we can work **HARDER** than we thought we could. This creates *strength*. Name something in life really worth having that doesn't require hard work. Even if we win the lottery or get lots of money from an inheritance, if we don't know the value of riches because we worked hard for them, we will most likely waste what is given to us.

3) We realize we can give **MORE** than we thought we could. This builds *character*. Working with hard workers is such a blessing. We learn that if they can keep going, we can keep going. And going further than we did before, giving more than we gave before, trying harder than we did before, this is what people of character do. I was reminded the other day that successful people put their shopping carts in the outdoor rack in the parking lot, take a little bit more time to do things right instead of being lazy and making others' jobs more difficult. Do more. It's a good way to live.

But what happens if we labor, and labor hard, and still fail? What if we gave our best but our livestock dies? What if we worked fingers to the bone but the crop fails? What if we gave our best but got laid off or demoted? What if we did our very best but the kids in our class still didn't care?

We always learn something from failure. Maybe we thought we gave our best but really didn't. Maybe we thought something was a good idea but it wasn't. Maybe we needed to grow in our ability or our ideas until we could make them work. Examples in history are legion of people who "failed" at different things but developed character, continued to labor, and finally had the labor rewarded. Abraham Lincoln is a favorite American hero who failed numerous times, but today is considered one of the greatest Americans of all time. Winston Churchill, despite being named the "Person of the Century" for the 1900's, failed a number of times in his life, including in his bid for re-election after WWII. He said "...failure is not fatal; it is the courage to continue that counts. Success is stumbling from failure to failure with no loss of enthusiasm."[14] Henry Ford said "Failure is only the opportunity to begin again; only this time more wisely."[15] So remember, as the Scripture says, *"In all labor there is profit..."* Labor on, then, and learn.

When the Storm Comes

I found an interesting article recently from Manila in the Philippines.[16] They had a strong typhoon knock out their power and threaten their food crops with winds upwards of 158 mph. It was their harvest season for rice and corn, their main staples. Governor Ben Evardone of the eastern province said it was a "double whammy", because the island had more than 11,600 COVID-19 cases and 772 deaths when the storm hit. The Philippines is no stranger to cyclones. It is considered a "natural disaster-prone country", with twenty or more typhoons passing near it or hitting it every year during the spring season.

So you have to wonder; how prepared are the people of the Philippines for these recurring natural disasters? I would think if you lived in the Philippines you would understand that storms are going to come, strong storms, storms that can threaten house and crops and life.

I assume Filipinos have stored up extra food, have shelters prepared in which they can hide, and emergency provisions like generators to produce their own electricity when the main lines are brought down. It's like living in Florida or Louisiana or Houston. You know another hurricane is going to come. You just don't know when.

And in the middle of the hurricane is not a great time to plan for emergencies. The planning and preparation must happen when the sun is shining and the wind isn't blowing too hard. Those plans and preparations may take months and even years to perfect, all for the relatively short time the storm is here. It's also hard when there is a "double whammy," as the governor described it, a double emergency for which you are unprepared. There are some things you can't plan for.

But there are a lot of things for which you can prepare. Americans who had cash reserves for home or business have been able to weather the COVID-19 storm better. People with a cellar are ready to run for shelter when the tornado is sighted. Extra food, water, flashlights, generators, first-aid kits, and the like are great to have when disaster strikes, because when it comes you may go to the store and find all the toilet paper and hand-sanitizer missing from the shelves.

We are warned many times in life to prepare. But when the sun shines and there's no storm we think we will be alright. We are like the grasshopper that made fun of the ant for working so hard, only to find out in winter it's a good thing to have stores of food laid by. That ant looks pretty smart now. Maybe we've been awakened a bit in our country to prepare; prepare physically, emotionally, and spiritually. One thing's for certain; another storm is always on the way, and once it arrives it's a bad time to try and do something about it. The time to prepare is while the weather is clear.

Whose Responsibility?

There are some things that only God can do. It is also true that we should thank Him for the strength to help us do what He commands us to do. It is our job to...

Stand firm in the work of the Lord (I Corinthians 15:58)

Work hard as unto the Lord (Colossians 3:23)

Bear your load; don't be a loafer (Galatians 6:5) and bear other's burdens (Galatians 6:2)

Keep sowing in faith (Galatians 6:7)

Show your good works to others (James 2:26)

Look after the needy (James 1:27)

Be faithful in assigned tasks (Matthew 25:21)

The commands of the Old Testament were attached to blessings for obedience and penalties for disobedience; in other words, the Law emphasized the responsibility of individuals to respond in morally appropriate ways to God's revealed truth. God clearly told them what He wanted, and He expected them to do what He told them. He told Cain that sin crouched at the door and wanted to take him, but that he was responsible to master it. (Genesis 3)

Achan sinned, and was held responsible. Jonah sinned, and God sent a storm to get his attention so he would do his duty. Elders and deacons and pastors are held accountable for the responsibilities God gives them. Humans like to avoid responsibility at times by blame-shifting. Adam and Eve did so. Saul tried it. Pilate tried it. Our instinctive reaction to being accused of something is to point the finger at another and say, "Not my fault; it's them!"

God won't hear of it. He has clearly told us in the Bible what our responsibilities are. Let us seek to fulfill them by His grace, for His glory.

Yeah

I once had a wonderful young man who was in my Sunday school class when he was in the 3rd, 4th, and 5th grade. We often did morning services led by our children during those days, where we asked students to lead the music, lead a responsive reading, take the offering, or help read a prepared script for the preaching part of the service. Nearly all the children were willing to do whatever asked, but Brenden was especially eager to fill in wherever needed.

"Hey Brenden, will you lead the music for the service?"

"Yeah."

"Hey Brenden, will you be a part of this presentation?"

"Yeah."

"Hey, Brenden, will you help take the offering and lead the prayer?"

"Yeah."

I was so impressed by his willingness to take whatever task we assigned without complaining or making excuses. It's hard to find a fifty-year-old who is so eager to serve; but to find a ten-year-old like that, it's special. I was convicted myself about my own willingness to do whatever God wanted me to do. Brenden's answer was always "yeah", but was mine? I couldn't always say that it was.

It's a simple but profound idea—when the Lord asks us to step up, will we instantly and gladly tell Him we will? When we become Christians we must die to self, which means that in essence the Lord gives us a blank contract and bids us sign at the bottom, *not knowing* what all He might ask of us, but being *ready* to step in *wherever* we are needed. The Lord doesn't have to tell us right then what He will ask of us. It is enough to know that we are signing up for whatever and whenever. Brenden's story is such a good one I just wanted to share it.

There's another reason to share it today as well. Brenden, now a young man, was ordained as a pastor yesterday. Anyone surprised? God can do a lot with a person who says "yeah" when asked to do something for Him.

Chapter Two—
Perseverance

The previous chapter was about character, and perseverance could fit there. But it is so important a character quality that I found I had written and thought a lot about it, and so gave it a chapter of its own. When I was young I found that I was weak in persevering, and so I have meditated much on improving this quality in myself. Paul didn't want to preach to others and then be found lacking, and I don't want to either. The Bible had a lot to say about perseverance and endurance. It is in human nature to want to quit when things get hard. And things often do get hard. Life is a series of ups and downs, much like a roller coaster. I'm not sure how it's possible that there are more downs than ups, but it sure seems that way at times. Here are stories of folks that didn't give up, but kept on going to a better place. This kind of attitude can one day result in our joining the apostle Paul who said he had fought a good fight and finished his race to the end. (II Timothy 4:7)

A Guy Who Wouldn't Quit

Karoly Takacs was a championship marksman with a pistol. In 1938, already having won numerous national and international 25-meter rapid-fire pistol competitions, he set his sights on the 1940 Tokyo Olympic games. He had been one of his country's greatest chances for a medal in the 1936 games in Berlin, but was disqualified because he was only a sergeant in the army, and Hungary only allowed commissioned officers to take part. Sadly, during an army training exercise in 1938 a grenade exploded in Takacs right hand and completely destroyed it.

Most people would have quit, but not Takacs. Even though he was right-handed, he began to shoot with his left. Within one year he had become so good that he competed in the Hungarian national shooting championship and won it. Then came World War II, and the Olympic Games were cancelled for 1940 and 1944. Takacs continued to practice, and in 1948 won the gold medal at the Games, beating the reigning world champion. He won again in 1952, the first athlete to win back-to-back gold medals in this event. He also turned his knowledge and perseverance into coaching, and helped a fellow Hungarian win a silver medal in the Olympics.

His endurance and grit won him an "Olympic hero" status from the International Olympic Committee. Karoly Takacs proved himself to not only be an Olympic champion, but one who illustrated perseverance of Olympian proportions.[17]

How Can I?

Since the carnage of WWII brought the need for heart surgery to a critical point, surgeons worked furiously in the 1940's to develop a heart-lung machine. At the beginning none of them were very good. They leaked blood, destroyed blood cells, and caused oxygen bubbles in the blood that killed patients. One of the pioneers, Dr. Given, developed a machine the size of a baby-grand piano, but it would only support the circulation of a cat eight inches long, and it had major problems. The most important problem during those early days was removing bubbles from the blood, because they would break capillaries and block blood flow to the heart. How could they bubble oxygen into the blood without creating bubbles in the blood? The best minds in surgery couldn't figure it out.

They gave the task of solving the problem to a young doctor named Dick DeWall. After pondering the situation, his solution was remarkably simple. He used an anti-foam chemical from a mayonnaise manufacturer to remove the bubbles.[18]

At about the same time in history, late in 1943, Edwin Land had been through a difficult and stressful time at work. He was on vacation with his family, walking the streets of Santa Fe, New Mexico, with his daughter Jennifer. An inch of snow on the ground, the smell of pine in the air, the walk was wonderfully restorative. They stopped near a landmark so Edwin could photograph Jennifer. After he clicked the shutter she cried "Let me see!" Edwin explained that she couldn't see the picture until the film was developed.

"Why not now?" Jennifer asked.

Why not now? Land thought.

It took thirty years and the combined efforts of many people, but the world was introduced in 1973 to the Polaroid "instant" camera. A whole new system of photographic chemistry had to be developed, as well as a new kind of camera engineered that contained the chemicals for development. But it wasn't impossible, and people of that era (including me) saw their pictures develop right before their eyes.[19]

Don't say "I can't." Ask, "How can I?" Make it your mission in life to have a new mind-set and use a new language. Resign rotten thinking and talking and ask "How can I solve this problem?" Some things may be impossible; but many things aren't impossible. They just have to be approached in the right way, and it's our job to figure out the answer.

Is it Worth It?

Stephen Ambrose, in his best-selling book *Band of Brothers*, notes that every man who entered battle suffered wounds. Many of the wounds were physical—lost limbs and deep physical scars—but all of the men had mental and emotional wounds as well. One of the commanding officers of those battles says, "I'm not sure that anybody who lived through [battle] hasn't carried with him, in some hidden ways, the scars. Perhaps that is the factor that helps keep Easy men bonded so unusually close together."

They knew each other at a level only those who have fought together can know. They had endured the suffering of extreme cold, insufficient food, little sleep, and the constant tension of men doing their utmost to kill you. And they had one more fear—the fear that it was all for nothing. One of the combat veterans wrote later in his life, "The deepest fear of my war years, one still with me, is that these happenings had no real purpose...How often I wrote in my war journals that unless that day had some positive significance for my future life, it could not possibly be worth the pain it cost."[20]

Most of us have not faced physical combat like these men did. But we all have spiritual combat experience if we know the Lord. We have a real enemy, sworn to bring death and destruction to our lives. We have faced him many times, and we have the scars to prove it. Nobody exits this life without battle scars, and if you have lived many years you will have many of them. But we must know that the battle is part of God's purpose for our lives, and that it is worth the struggle.

When I was growing up there was a song called *It Will Be Worth it All*. The words are comforting...

> *"Sometimes the day seems long, our trials hard to bear. We're tempted to complain, to murmur and despair. But Christ will soon appear to catch His bride away! All tears forever over in God's eternal day! It will be worth it all when we see Jesus. Life's trials will seem so small, when we see Christ. One glimpse of His dear face all sorrows will erase, so bravely run the race 'til we see Christ."*

Since the God of battles ordains that spiritual warfare is part of our life's journey, endure the hardships, fight the good fight, and keep in mind that for God's glory and our sanctification, our struggles are worth it. One way it is worth the battles is that it bonds you to other believers in a way the world cannot understand. And one day, for enduring in faith to the end, you will hear the Father say, "Well done!"

It Never Hurts to Ask

I, like many, have acted the fool many times in my life. When I was growing up I somehow believed that every male on the planet understood some things I didn't get; that they knew how to fix broken vehicles, build houses, repair lawnmowers, and do all those "manly" things; but in some inexplicable way I was left out of this knowledge. In many ways I was a tremendously secure individual, and I thank the Lord and my loving parents for that gift. But with machines and construction and repairing things, I was definitely insecure, and so I was afraid to ask.

My brother was much wiser. When he was in high school he came home one day and said he got a job at a gas station. My response was, "But you don't know anything about working at a gas station." He, being much smarter than I, replied, "Exactly—that's why I want the job—so I can learn." The next year his summer job was on a construction crew for the same reason.

Meanwhile, I worked at McDonald's. Nothing wrong with learning to cook a burger, but I missed out on great learning opportunities in other fields. I was afraid I would look like a doofus since I didn't know anything. In reality I was a doofus, not for being ignorant, but for not asking.

It took me until about the age of 38 to realize a couple of things: I was definitely not the only male of the species who couldn't repair a car or lawnmower, and the dumbest way to go through life was refusing to ask questions. I belatedly asked people to show me how to do some things, and I became more skilled at them. I helped build our church kitchen and a great friend showed me many things about construction. With his advice and help I built a game room and garage. The building isn't perfect, but it's still standing, and I learned the builder's secret:

there is a reason for trim—it helps cover the mistakes. (By the way, that's why in my game room I used *wide* trim.)

I'm so glad I finally learned that you don't have to know it all. Asking questions and getting good answers is a part of life. It doesn't mean you are dumb. It's dumb to pretend you know something when you obviously don't; and even dumber to never learn by refusing to ask someone smarter than you.

No Rest for the Warriors

The First Infantry Division already had a long and distinguished history before World War II began. Their work was so respected they were given a prominent role in *Operation Torch*, the amphibious assault against North Africa that began the U.S. military's active battle presence in the war. In that assault they acquitted themselves well. So they were chosen to participate in the amphibious assault of Sicily in July 1943, *Operation Husky*. There they were able to wrestle control of the island from Fascist Italy and Nazi Germany and force enemy withdrawal onto mainland Italy. By the time these two operations were over the boys of the Fighting First were understandably ready for rest and relaxation, even a return home to the States.

But Omar Bradley and the rest of the Allied general officers were looking for a veteran amphibious assault division, one with experience at facing enemy guns along a shoreline, because they had another amphibious assault in mind, *Operation Overlord*, the invasion of France. There was only one division like that, The Big Red One, as the Fighting First was called.

Lieutenant Colonel Bill Gara, commanding officer of the 1st Engineer Combat Battalion, remembered the grumbling. "The men were saying 'we're ready to go home now—we've done our share—get somebody else to do it.'" Originally the First wasn't considered for *Overlord*, but they were too good at what they did, and the operation was too important not to use them. Some of the other assault forces were green, so a veteran group was needed to show them how it was done. They were shipped from the Mediterranean to England, trained for months, then spearheaded the most ambitious sea assault ever attempted in the history of war against the most prepared defenses ever seen.

The rest is history. The Fighting First assaulted Omaha Beach on June 6, 1944, and over 2400 Americans lost their lives in the bloody struggle. There were countless acts of heroism that day among the men of the First, including a young soldier named Eldon Wiehe, with the 1st Artillery. Separated from the rest of his unit, nearly hit by a German shell, he fell apart, panicked, and started crying. A landing craft had run aground, so some friends escorted him to relative safety behind it. "I cried for what seemed like hours, until tears would no longer come. Suddenly, I felt something. I can't explain it, but a feeling went through my body and I stopped crying and came to my senses." He picked up his rifle and rejoined the war, conquering his worst fears. It's a heroic thing to conquer self.

And then there was Private Carlton Barrett, who won the Medal of Honor that day, returning to the killing fields in the surf again and again to assist buddies onto the shore and up to the relative safety of the shingle. The barrage of machine gun fire, small arms fire, and mortar attack was unbelievable, but Barrett "assisted the wounded; calmed the shocked; arose as a leader in the stress of the occasion." He constantly risked his own life and safety for many hours to help his friends, which had "an inestimable effect on his comrades," according to his citation.[21]

If you are a believer, you have been called to combat. It is understandable that if you are a veteran, you long for ease, home, and retirement from the struggle. But the battles rage on, and because you are a veteran you are needed by those less experienced. It is your task to risk yourself, to give yourself away, to conquer your own fears and doubts, and to help others in their fight. Rest only comes when life is over, and the war against our arch-enemy is won.

No You Don't!!

If you've seen the Kendrick Brothers movie *War Room*, there is a scene where the woman who was a feisty prayer warrior refuses to allow her purse to be stolen. She stands up to the thief. The identical scenario was played out in the life of a woman I know, a woman small in stature but large in character and spunk.

This woman barely stands five feet tall (she claims) and at the time of the incident couldn't have weighed much over a hundred pounds, but a would-be thief tried to grab her purse as she was opening the trunk of her car one day in the big city. Instead of being intimidated she indignantly yelled at the man, "No, you don't! You will *not* take my purse." They engaged in a very brief tug-of-war, which she won, and the thief was frightened off.

What a beautiful illustration of James 4:7. That precious promise says you are to do two things in life to be successful in spiritual warfare: you are to *submit* to God, and you are to *resist* the devil. Submitting to God is how you get saved, and it's how you walk with Him. Micah 6:8 tells us that part of what is good and what God requires of you is to walk humbly with God.

But the second part of James 4:7 is important too, and sometimes we fail in obeying that injunction. Do we resist the devil like the small woman resisted the thief? Do we say NO to him, in a loud and affronted voice? Far too often Satan attacks us, and instead of confronting him and resisting him, knowing that in Christ we have victory, we meekly allow him to bully us. It's as though we say "Here comes the devil...I'm whipped now."

A thousand times NO!! God has not given us a spirit of fear, but of *power* and love and a sound mind. We should not only command Satan to leave us and our loves ones alone, but we should *expect* him to go. Many Christians act like the command said "resist God and submit to the devil". They've got it all backwards. When we submit our lives to God Proverbs 28:1 says we should be bold as a lion. So when the old lion Satan prowls around, seeking whom he may devour, just remember, growl back. He is a coward at heart. The Lord promises he will flee if you just stand up to him and say, *"NO YOU DON'T!"*

Sunset's Promise

Have you ever noticed that if you are looking at a picture you can't tell if it is a picture of a sunrise or sunset? You don't know if the camera was pointing east or west. Beautiful pictures are one or the other, a dawning or a sunset, but you don't know which.

How profound. We sometimes dread the closing of a day. It means darkness falls, and with it perhaps fears and anxieties arise to plague us. We've all had hard nights where we had fearful dreams that woke us up, and we couldn't help but be bombarded with horrible thoughts about what might happen that made us fearful. Then the morning sun rose, and much of the fear dissipated with the coming of light. We find ourselves ready to meet the challenges of the new day, and the worries recede.

We must remember that the setting of one sun just means a dark interlude resulting in the rising of another sun. A new day cannot dawn unless the former day ends. What hope the new day brings! Let the old day with its sorrows depart, and let the new day arise. We do not know the evening before what great things the next day will bring; what answers to prayer; what promises fulfilled; what joys experienced. Rather than face the end of the day with sadness, let us thank God for taking us through it, and rejoice at what He will do when the sun rises again.

One Step at a Time

I had climbed the highest peak in Colorado, Mt. Elbert. I had climbed the highest peak in Texas, Guadalupe Peak. It was time to climb the highest peak in New Mexico, Wheeler Peak. On the first two climbs my son Stephen had been along as trail guide, and believe me, it was hard to keep up with him. Thirty-one years my junior and very athletic, he seemed to flow up the inclines as I huffed and puffed to make it to the end. Stephen was going for this assault on Wheeler as well, and so was my daughter Deborah and my youngest son, Josiah. Josiah was eleven-years-old and I figured it was high time he experienced the thrill of setting and reaching a tough goal. It was seven and a half miles up, seven and a half miles back down. Not a particularly easy hike for any of us.

We started early on a gorgeous June morning, and found ourselves right on schedule, enjoying God's creation and each other. Stephen was in his late twenties, Deborah in her late teens, both of them in considerably better shape than Dad and Josiah. They kept a brisk pace, and we kept falling behind. We had traversed about six miles of our journey when Josiah decided he'd had enough. Stephen and Deborah were 200 yards ahead of us, and Josiah collapsed on the ground. "I can't make it!" he moaned. Rather fatigued myself, I told him that we were "almost" there, that he and I didn't have to keep up with the other two, and we would just proceed more slowly. "We can make it."

Slowly he gathered his emotions and his breath, and we started off again. Stephen and Deborah had in the meantime come back to check on us, given Josiah encouragement, and then promptly moved ahead at a much faster pace than Josiah and I could maintain. After another half mile or so Josiah wanted to give in again. "Dad, I can't make it. I don't want to quit but I just can't go on." It brought to mind my climb with Stephen up Mt. Elbert in Colorado a couple of years earlier. I had told Stephen that I couldn't make it all the way to the top; that I was satisfied with being within a thousand feet of the summit, but he had refused to hear it. "No, Dad, you'll make it, just keep on going. We're almost there." Well, somehow I found the strength to endure and was very happy to complete the climb and buy the t-shirt. Proverbs 13:12 says hope deferred makes the heart sick, but when the desire comes (when the goal is reached) it brings a tree of life. We are happiest when we conquer ourselves and reach the goal we've set.

So that day on Wheeler I reminded Josiah of the principle, and told him, "It may take us all day to get there. You don't have to go fast, and you can stop as many times as you need to stop, but I'm with you all the way, and we are going to make it to the top." I helped him up the slope we were on, and we continued. We stopped numerous times, and Josiah began to believe we would survive. A few hundred yards from the summit we stopped for the last time, and he said, "Dad, I know you are right. I'm glad I kept going."

We took our picture on the top of Wheeler Peak, jotted our names in the logbook there, and next to "age" I proudly put 59 ½. I was feeling pretty good about being an old man who could conquer the mountain and thought not many people my age could do this. We sat down to eat our lunch and along came another old codger. He looked like he might be about my age, so after chewing the fat for a couple of minutes I ventured, "If you don't mind telling me, how old are you?" "70" was the reply. Boy was I deflated! I've got to keep hiking up mountains another eleven years to match him! And then I realized that the lesson Josiah and I had learned was one that carries into every aspect of life and for all of life. We should never stop making worthy goals, or taking one step at a time to see them accomplished. Thank God we have earthly guides and peers that spur us on when we think we're too tired to make it all the way. I was so proud of Josiah that day. He conquered himself. It's one of the greatest goals you can achieve.

We made it to the top!

The Blue Line

Eons ago, when I coached high school basketball, we would run wind sprints, as all teams do. You know the drill; run to the free throw line and back, to half court and back, to the opposite free throw line and back. The word basketball in the Greek language is translated "run between the lines a lot."

We've all done it if we've played basketball, and every coach knows that his or her team will not be in shape if they don't run a bunch between the lines. Vince Lombardi said fatigue makes cowards of us all[22], and so a coach wants the players to face their cowardice and overcome it. In our gym the end line was blue. At the end of each rep of "jingle jangles" or running back and forth, the players were to sprint as hard as they could from the opposite end line back to the starting point, the blue line.

Chapter Two—Perseverance

When I coached I urged my players to run *through* the blue line. I had noticed that in nearly all the boys there was a tendency to let up and coast the last few steps as they neared the finish line. After all, they were just nearly done with that set, and they wanted to ease in, like they would break or something if they didn't go all out until the end. "Think like a champion. Don't ease up the last ten feet. Don't cheat yourself and your teammate. Run through the blue line."

I was reminded of this today. I am past the stage of my life where running wind sprints is a good idea. My knees can't take it, and I am reminded that I really don't want knee surgery if I can possibly help it. But walking is a great idea for somebody my age, so I've been walking. Today it was cold and dreary, and I didn't really feel like getting out there to walk; but I thankfully had the discipline to bundle up and set off. I had a particular goal in mind of the distance for my walk, but I was tempted several times to turn around early and head for home without reaching the goal. After all, I certainly deserved it. I had walked further than my goal last week, and the week before that. And I would have time to walk further tomorrow. I had all kinds of reasons why stopping short was acceptable.

But I didn't do it. I was reminded of all those times in all those practices where I had urged all those guys to give their best, to finish strong, to not cheat themselves or those who were counting on them. Well, what's good for the players is good for the coach. When I stop short I not only cheat myself, but I cheat my spouse, my children, my grandchildren, the people in my church and community. I'm so glad that today I decided to walk through the blue line. Nobody is so old that there isn't a blue line somewhere they have to run past as they finish strong.

The Last Step

Well yesterday was the last step of a forty-year career in education. Hard to believe. I remember about seven years ago preparing to hike a mountain with my oldest sons. I figured the best preparation was simply to walk, and walk, and walk some more. I walked four or five times a week, logging many miles, and as I did I noticed the time a person has to think on such journeys. My life has always been such a hurry, scurry thing it was rather jarring to slow down so much. You can't walk five or ten miles in just a few minutes, so there was ample time for reflection.

I thought about so many things, but my mind often came back to comparing my life and career to a long walk. I ran different scenarios through my mind about how much longer I would teach, how the finances would work once I retired, what kinds of things I would do once the teaching days were over, and a host of other issues I would face. When you've already walked four or five miles, and you are a bit weary, you sometimes feel like you won't have the strength to finish, to get back home, because you still have several miles left in your journey. It was the same way for me in considering retirement in those days. I had already completed well over thirty years of my life trying to knock out ignorance and prepare students for college, and I wondered how much longer I could keep it up.

In the physical walk you realize that the secret to longevity and success is pretty simple. Just focus on what you are doing at the moment. Just think about the next step, and the next, and the next. It may be boring, but ultimately it gets you to your destination. You realize that you can't quit where you are yet, because you are not home. Finishing a career turned out to be the same concept. I just kept on walking, one day at a time, one class at a time, one project or lesson plan at a time, until I was done.

And back of it all is the strength that God provides. I love the story of Caleb in the bible. Here was a young man who arrived at the Promised Land ready to tackle the giants, but his comrades' lack of faith caused him to walk in the wilderness for forty years. Did he succumb to depression and fear? On the contrary, he took a million steps one at a time, and when he returned, he said he was as strong as the day he left, ready to conquer his mountain. Only God can give you that kind of inner strength. Well, I praise Him for strengthening me in a similar way over these forty years, and I anticipate a continued supply of strength. Because one thing is for certain; no matter how long the journey, the last step of that journey only means there will be a first step into the next journey. Until heaven is our home, we're not home yet, and there's more walking (and fighting) to do.

Chapter Three—
History Lessons

Hegel is credited with first saying that the only thing we learn from history is that we learn nothing from history.[23] There is a lot of truth to the saying, but the wise should at least *try* to learn. When I was young I loved fictional adventure stories, stories like *Treasure Island, White Fang,* the books of Jules Verne, and the like. As I have aged I have enjoyed reading real life adventure stories, and lessons from real historical figures. Many of these figures showed incredible character and resilience. Others were extraordinarily foolish and we are warned by their mistakes. Some of my musings from the pages of history are found in this chapter. I have a strong desire to imitate the heroic figures from the past, and to likewise avoid the pitfalls and subsequent heartaches of those who floundered in the big moments. Let's prove Hegel wrong and learn something from history, shall we?

A Triumph of Virtue

George Washington was discouraged. His men had lost the battles of Brandywine and Germantown despite his best efforts to rally and inspire them, and his biggest rival, General Horatio Gates, had trounced British General John Burgoyne at Saratoga (although Benedict Arnold, of all people, was the catalyst and hero of the victorious battle). Gates, a puffed-up, arrogant man, began to strut about like a cocky rooster and position himself to replace Washington as commander-in-chief.

Several in the Continental Congress were mulling just such a move, and this juxtaposition of defeat versus victory increased the discontent with Washington's leadership. Serious questions began to arise about whether Washington was up to the job.

Discontent increased when another preening, self-serving officer, Thomas Conway, was considered for promotion to major general. Conway was a fortune hunter who had written that his motivation for joining the revolutionary army was so he could be promoted and "cash in on the fight." Conway's evaluation of Washington's abilities as a general was that his skills were "miserable indeed." To add insult to injury, one of Washington's former aides, Thomas Mifflin, a man whom Washington had befriended, was also working to see Washington removed from his duties as commander. Congressmen were also conspiring against him. Jonathan Dickinson Sergeant said Washington's defeats were unnecessary and a "disgrace." Richard Henry Lee helped reorganize the board of war and made sure Mifflin was placed on it (ultimately they got General Gates to be its head). Even Washington's friend Dr. Benjamin Rush sided against the commander in chief. Some congressmen believed Washington was too praised by too many, and as congressman Lovell opined, these machinations were intended to "rap a demigod over the knuckles."

So how to deal with this backstabbing, grasping lot? Washington perhaps was no very great battle strategist, but his political skills were sublime. Derogatory letters written by generals Conway and Gates had fallen into Washington's hands. He responded by sending them both a copy of the letters without comment. His silence was very powerful, and both men were flustered, returning letters to Washington that tried to cover their misdeeds and lay the blame elsewhere. Washington was cold to his adversaries, but treated them with respect when he had to see them in public. He also, for the sake of unity in the army, refrained from telling tales indiscreetly or publicly defaming his foes. Historian Ron Chernow says Washington had command of his tongue and his temper, and that through it all he was "dignified, circumspect, and upright, whereas his enemies seemed petty and skulking."[24]

Even crusty old John Adams, often critical of Washington himself, lauded Washington's self-control during the "Conway Cabal". He realized that Washington was the main unifying figure in the war, and that despite Washington's faults, he should be supported and followed. As Chernow says, "In the last analysis, Washington's triumph over the troublesome Gates, Mifflin, and Conway was total." Mifflin resigned over allegations of misconduct; Gates' own defects as a general became clear to everyone over time; and Conway, despite continuing to harangue Washington for some time, eventually apologized for his poor treatment of him and called Washington "a great and good man." He finished a final letter to Washington by saying "May you long enjoy the love, veneration, and esteem of these states whose liberties you have asserted by your virtues." Washington indeed had virtue, as opposed to his naysayers. It's nice to see the good guy in politics win out once in a while.

Fatal Philosophy

"What is moral is what you feel good after, and what is immoral is what you feel bad after." [25]

This is the mantra of many Americans today. It contains the narcissism and entitlement too common in our nation. When you become the sole arbiter of right and wrong, moral or immoral behavior, you tread on very thin ice.

Could it be that the thief feels pretty good after getting away with his loot, or that the philanderer feels pretty good about dodging his wife to be with his mistress, or that Jeffrey Epstein felt pretty good about trafficking all those young girls on his pleasure island? It's even possible that the murderer felt good after he killed his victim, especially if had sufficient loathing for that victim.

Our Founding Fathers understood that unless we are governed by an external moral compass we are undone. Some things are inherently right, and some inherently wrong, despite what we feel about them. Benjamin Rush and John Adams, both integral Founders, were lamenting the loss of morals among young people in their day, after the founding of the country. Rush wrote to Adams, *"By renouncing the Bible, philosophers swing from their moorings upon all moral subjects...it is the only correct map of the human heart that has ever been published."*[26] Adams agreed, and responded, *"The Bible contains the most profound philosophy, the most perfect morality, and the most refined policy that ever was conceived on earth...Without national morality a republican government cannot be maintained."*[27] It would be a nice lesson for the rioters in our nation to learn; that torching businesses and destroying police cars and beating people senseless or shooting them to death is not, and never will be right, no matter what group is doing the burning, destroying, beating, and shooting.

The opening quote is illustrative of the life of moral emptiness so prevalent in our own day, what the Bible calls "vain philosophy and empty deceit" (Colossians 2:8). It was made by a man who had incredible success by the world's standards; winning a Pulitzer Prize and a Nobel Prize for Literature in back-to-back years. He was admired by many for his large lifestyle, and he had money, fame, a career that dramatically influenced his field, and he was mourned when he died. A successful life? Hardly. Married four times, growing increasingly neurotic as he aged, paranoid, and anxious, he could not be helped. He spent time in the Mayo Clinic and other healthcare facilities, treated for his mental disintegration, all to no avail. On July 2, 1961, Ernest Hemingway killed himself with the shotgun he had used on many of his hunting expeditions.[28]

No wonder. When you refuse to submit to God's truths about your condition, you are left with...what? Yourself as the sole guide for your "morality?" Wonder if Hemingway "felt good" after he pulled the trigger and went on his journey to meet his Creator.

Chapter Three—History Lessons

Friends Indeed

James Shields was handsome, thin-skinned, with a touch of arrogance. He was the Illinois state auditor, a public figure, a man who at times deserved public criticism. But this was going too far. There were anonymous letters supposedly from him placed in the Sagamon Journal, and everyone in Illinois laughed at the bitingly sarcastic notes. One missive said, "Dear girls, it is distressing, but I cannot marry you all. Too well I know how you suffer; but do, *do* remember, it is not my fault that I am so handsome and so interesting."

Everyone laughed, except Shields. He obviously didn't think the letters so funny; and he finally did something about it, sending a friend to demand of the editor the name of the person responsible. One man in the cabal, the driving force behind the skewering, was now troubled. "I only meant it as a joke, but now I've involved myself, and, what's worse, others too." So the man who had done an ignoble thing decided to do a noble thing. Without disclosing the names of the other conspirators, he confessed and took sole responsibility for the calamity.

Shields challenged him to a duel. As the challenged party, our friend had the choice of weapons, but he was terrible with a pistol and almost every other weapon he could think of. One thing he'd had a bit of experience using was the broadsword; so he decided on these as the dueling pieces. Since it was a crime in Illinois to duel, the combatants went to Missouri, three days hard ride away. The contestants and seconds placed the time and place, and our man, full of apprehension and woe, made his way to the field of battle.

Thankfully the man had friends who realized what a disaster was impending, and they rode like maniacs to reach the combatants before they could do serious damage to one another. They pleaded with them to cease and desist, and our man did a second noble thing: he abjectly apologized for causing this stain on Shields' character and for instigating the whole sorry mess. Shields tactfully received the apology, and no duel ensued. It was a critical moment in the life of our hero. Had he gone through with the duel he might have been maimed or killed. His future political hopes would certainly have been dashed. It was a good thing that they weren't dashed. The man who had caused all the trouble was Abraham Lincoln.

This wasn't the first time Lincoln had used his droll wit to attack others using anonymous letters, but it certainly was the last. He learned his lesson, and despite receiving more criticism than any other president, he never lashed out in retaliation. I'm sure Lincoln often thanked the Lord for those friends who rescued him from his own folly. Lincoln showed humility and wisdom in apologizing to Shields, and Shields showed magnanimity in accepting the apology. Lincoln became our most admired president; but it would not have happened had not three friends ridden hard all day and night to appeal to his good senses.[29]

May every one of us be blessed with a friend who will confront us when we are being foolish, and may we have the grace of God to recognize our foolishness and turn to wisdom. This story is perhaps the foundation of this endearing Lincoln quote: "The better part of one's life consists of his friendships." [30]

Glory and Fame

Since my earliest days I've enjoyed a good book. In upper grade school and junior high I migrated to adventure and animal stories, like most guys who loved to read. During my later high school years and into college and young adulthood I sadly found less time to read for pleasure as my responsibilities grew. When I found the time I read textbooks and books about faith for the most part. As I've aged I've become interested in biographies, the adventures and life stories of people who accomplished or survived remarkable things. Truth is not only stranger than fiction, it's much more fun to know that some fantastic things really happened and aren't the figment of someone's overactive imagination.

I've just finished four books about famous people, and noticed a common theme in the lives of John F. and Jackie Kennedy, Charles

Lindbergh, John Wooden, and Steve McQueen. I was reminded of how entitled and narcissistic JFK was, and how he philandered much even though he had a glamorous trophy wife. I hadn't realized how famous Charles Lindbergh was for his time, of his mercurial rise from quiet loner that few knew to literally the most photographed and recognized face on planet earth. John Wooden was a fascinating read for me since his UCLA Bruin basketball teams won ten national championships in twelve years during my formative years. I have admired him and his ability to produce winners so consistently. And then there's Steve McQueen, the highest paid movie star during the 60's and 70's, a man I knew little about.

What was the connecting link between them all? All of them, during their time and after, were and are household names. Adults my age know them all, and probably know something about them. They accomplished amazing things in their lives, two of them dying relatively young and two living to ripe old age. But another common thread was what they discovered about fame. JFK relished it but still wanted his privacy (though a serial womanizer he actually was an affectionate father). Lindbergh hated the publicity, the paparazzi, and it made for him a long and fairly miserable life trying to escape the notoriety. Wooden enjoyed the championships to be sure, but he said many times that he enjoyed his non-championship teams just as much, and that the pressure of winning another ring was so difficult to handle that it soured much of the experience. McQueen went from nobody to TV star in *"Wanted: Dead or Alive"*, then rocketed to moviestardom in *"The Magnificent Seven"* and *"The Great Escape."* It all took only ten years and nearly destroyed his life (as so many other Hollywood icons have discovered).

Wooden was a Christian and dedicated husband, and so he was able to keep his moral compass and survive his fame. McQueen near the end of his short life (he died at 50) found Christ, six months before he was diagnosed with mesothelioma (from exposure to asbestos), so even though the last year of his life was extremely hard and painful, he died in peace knowing his eternal destination. Kennedy died during the heyday of Camelot, unaware of how short life is and how much he did to ignore the real meaning of his existence.

All of them climbed the mountain and found out this one inescapable truth: when you get to the top, there's nothing there. McQueen, like so many, found that money, fame, sex, drugs, and stardom never could fill the void that only God can fill. Lindbergh moved his family to England to escape the United States press, who hounded him unmercifully. In some ways I think he wished he had never made his famous flight. Wooden enjoyed his years after coaching more than the years he was coaching undefeated champions (he did it four times in that 12-year stretch between 1963 and 1975).

Why do so many sell their souls for fame and glory? The only glory that satisfies is living a life for the glory of God, and the only fame worth anything is simply to hear Him say at the end, "Well done, good and faithful servant." (Matthew 25:23)

Here to Stay

The young West Point cadet reported to school looking like a vagabond. His figure was angular and clumsy, his gait awkward. He was dressed in old-fashioned Virginia homespun woolen cloth, wearing a low-crowned, broad-brimmed woolen hat. On his shoulders he carried some old stained saddle bags. He looked like what he was, a poor bedraggled country boy.

Only three years of age when both his older sister and father died, his poor, ill mother remarried when he was five. He was farmed out to live with grandmother, but hated the idea of leaving his mother so much that he spent a night alone in the woods, and could only be bribed into leaving with promises of gifts. The time spent with his grandmother, aunts and uncles was a time of almost no schooling, unbridled freedom, and negative influences by the godless uncles who cared not a whit about the Ten Commandments or any other Bible verses for that matter. At age eleven he was sent away from this place of riotous living to a cousin's house, but he disagreed with the cousin's rules and returned to the uncles and scenes of poverty, debauchery, and drunkenness.

Finally at age fourteen, something happened to the boy. He reacted against the rowdy behavior and attitude of his uncles and became extremely serious about study. He also began to walk several miles each Sunday to listen to the local preacher's sermons. Now, his life on the straight and narrow, grown to age eighteen, he was at the premiere military school in the nation.

The young man had decided to become something, with God's help; so he marched into West Point dressed shabbily, but with an air about him that was immediately recognizable to those who observed him. Dabney Maury, at the time a cadet, but a man of keen eye who would become a general himself one day, wrote "He tramped along by the side of the sergeant, with an air of resolution, and his stolid look added to the inflexible determination of his whole aspect, so that one of us remarked, 'That fellow has come here to stay.'"

The young man did well at the academy, graduated and became a general, and one of the most colorful and competent leaders of men known to American history. He became known for his Christian faith and devotion, seeking to avoid battle on Sundays and encouraging his men to attend church services on that day. As a leader he was decisive and deceptive, able to maneuver his men into the right place at the right time for maximum effectiveness, and often fooling the enemy as to his whereabouts. In one of the early battles of the war he stationed his brigade in a strong line and resisted numerous attempts at breaking it, earning him his famous nickname.

"Stonewall" Jackson is considered by many military experts to be one of the greatest generals in American history. From poverty, heartache, and evil influences he rose to become something special, and he humbly gave credit to God for his success. When he arrived at West Point he arrived "to stay." That kind of determination and devotion is too often a rare attribute.

Like most very successful commanders, he was intensely focused and brave on the battlefield. A captain once remarked on this, to which

Stonewall said, "Captain, my religious belief teaches me to feel as safe in battle as in bed. God has fixed the time for my death. I do not concern myself about that, but to be always ready, no matter when it may overtake me. Captain, that is the way all men should live, and then all would be equally brave." [31]

May all of us live that way, and may all of us arrive to stay at our place of service and duty. The battle is never over until God calls us home.

Mentors

Everyone needs an older, wiser person; to give them counsel, to guide them when they are confused, to advise them on the proper way to proceed. Abraham Lincoln was blessed with several men who helped him become one of the greatest Americans of all. Andrew Crawford was the first mentor in young Lincoln's life. Abe went to school very infrequently as a boy, mostly because his father, Thomas, didn't have an education and saw no need for his son to have one. For a short period Crawford was Lincoln's teacher in a small country "blab" school, and he was the first to encourage the future president to expand his intellectual wings and reach for something bigger.

The second guiding hand in Abraham's journey was aptly named Mentor Graham.[32] Lincoln had decided to become a surveyor like his hero, George Washington, and Graham helped him study. They often burned the midnight oil, pouring over surveying and other books. Lincoln did become a surveyor, and was able to supplement his meager income this way.

Abe's final and most important mentor was Stephen T. Logan. Lincoln had been a lawyer for some time, and was a partner with John Stuart for the first few years, but that partnership had dissolved, and Logan asked Lincoln to join him. What Lincoln learned from Logan became such a strong part of his character that it helped him unknowingly prepare for the greatest set of debates in American history and Lincoln's entrance upon the national stage. Lincoln had always been a great storyteller; in fact, it was what most people associated with him. Storytelling came in handy in the courtroom of Lincoln's early law experience. Lincoln's wit and speaking skills helped him win cases. But Logan taught Lincoln the benefit of being methodical, painstaking, and precise when developing cases. Abe was amazed at how Logan could see through the forest to the trees, how he could come up with the single greatest weakness in his opponent's case and exploit it. Logan was never unprepared for an argument from a courtroom foe, and he had an answer for that argument.

Logan demanded the same attention to detail and preparation from his younger law partner. Lincoln turned from being a careless, sloppy jurist, to becoming a man of great preparation and competence.

Those character traits came in handy as Lincoln engaged Stephen A. Douglas in the debates of 1856 and 1858. Lincoln by that time had been able to discern the best way to not only defeat Douglas in the 1860 presidential race, but even more importantly, to gain national fame as the clearest voice against the expansion of slavery. Douglas, the wiliest and most able debater of the age, found himself facing a moral force from the Illinois plains in Lincoln. Lincoln is a man universally admired for his emancipation of the slaves and his wisdom, his ability to see beyond what others could see. I'm sure he would have credited his three great mentors, especially Stephen T. Logan, for their help in making him what he became. [10]

If your mentor is still alive today, thank them for the influence they have had in your life. Mentors give us wings and roots, invaluable tools to construct a godly life.

Not So Bad After All

Tall, white-haired, nearly seventy years of age, the celebrated orator took his place at the rostrum and delivered an epic two-hour speech on that cool November day. His high-flown rhetoric filled with quotes from the classics awed the crowd, the stentorian voice ringing out for the thousands who had gathered on this momentous and somber day, and his brilliant eloquence won the admiration of all those who attended the event. Prolonged applause ensued. Now it was time for another speech. Could the crowd stand another marathon of words? The second speaker took the podium and spoke in a sharp treble voice. The speech took about two minutes and was all of 272 words long. Some in the multitude had barely known a speech was being given when they realized it was all over.

The speaker was demonstrably disappointed in his effort. He told a friend, "It was a flat failure..." He wasn't the only one disheartened by the speech. A journalist from Chicago covering the event printed, "The cheek of every American must tingle in shame as he reads the silly, flat and dishwatery utterances of a man who has to be pointed out to foreigners as the President of the United States." The editor of the paper became even more vitriolic in his attack, saying of the words, "for the credit of the nation we are willing that the veil of oblivion shall be dropped over them and that they shall be no more repeated or thought of." Democrats of the day derided the speech as inadequate and inappropriate for the momentous occasion. Even some foreign journalists didn't like the speech, the *London Times* remarking that "The ceremony was made ludicrous" by the effort.

The speaker was dissatisfied, and some hearers weren't impressed, but once the truths shared in the speech sunk in, the vast majority of people realized that it was one of the greatest addresses ever given in the history of mankind. The speech, of course, was the Gettysburg Address, dedicating the cemetery where tens of thousands of Union and Confederate dead lay buried after that epic Civil War battle.

Edward Everett, the bombastic, long-winded speech-giver, wrote to Lincoln, "I should be glad if I could flatter myself that I came as near the central idea of the occasion, in two hours, as you did in two minutes." After Lincoln's death senator Charles Sumner said the Gettysburg Address was a "monumental act." He said Lincoln was mistaken that "the world will little note, nor long remember what we say here." "The world noted at once what he said, and will never cease to remember it. The battle itself was less important than the speech."

Historians have continued to marvel at the clarity of thought and universal themes expressed in the short speech. Leo Rosten said, "If a picture paints a thousand words, paint me the Gettysburg Address." *The London Times* of 1863 may not have liked the speech, but a modern paper from the UK calls it "the greatest speech in the world." [33] Abraham Lincoln is far and away the most quoted president in American history, and there are more references to quotes from his Gettysburg Address than from any other thing he said. It is this speech that is inscribed behind his imposing statue at the Lincoln Memorial in Washington, D.C.

Aren't we glad Lincoln didn't throw the speech away? When he gave it, he wasn't happy with it. But the world has been chewing on the ideas he presented for over 150 years. And few Americans know who Edward Everett was. Go ahead and give your best effort, and then let it go. You may not feel it is worth much, but somebody may find it inspiring nevertheless.

Not So Pretty

The Oklahoma farm boy was raised hardscrabble; and he didn't like it, always working hard and remaining poor. In 1925, on the brink of the Great Depression, he decided to rob the armored car carrying the Kroger grocery payroll. It was his first big crime, and he got hooked on the money, the excitement, the adventure of living large—as he saw it.

For years he would find himself afoul of the law, eventually killing men on two different occasions who tried to arrest him. Folks who knew him said he was the nicest young man you'd ever want to meet in some situations, generous to a fault with those he cared about. He tried to take care of his wife Ruby and their son Dempsey. But he also cheated on her frequently, couldn't tell the truth if his life depended on it, and although he often told others he wished he could just settle down and be home like normal folks, the problem wasn't the law chasing him, but the itching inside of him, the yen to travel, to steal, and to spend lavishly, to get away from the responsibilities of home and family. One long-time friend said you couldn't have made him settle down if you tied twenty anvils to his legs.

Like everyone else who finds themselves on the run, he finally tired of it. He once told Ruby, "Folks think that bank robbery is the road to riches…but it ain't." During his years of robbing banks he moved up the FBI's "Most Wanted" list until he became #1 after agent Melvin Purvis killed John Dillinger, knocking him from the top spot. Our man deeply hurt the two women who he said meant the most to him. Ruby often wept for days when he was gone and frequently was near starvation trying to care for herself and Dempsey. She alternately loved and hated her husband for his abandonment and infidelities, but she was as addicted to him as he was addicted to his wild existence. His mother too was grieved, naturally, at his lifestyle, and when he died she—like any other mother would have done—wept and commented that it wasn't natural to have to bury a beloved son.

Just before he was gunned down in an Ohio field, he spent several days in the deep woods, frantically running from the law, thinking about how much like a hunted animal he was. Charles Arthur Floyd died in a hail of bullets when he was just thirty-years-old, and many thousands of people attended his funeral.

One of his mistresses had given him the nickname "Pretty Boy", and it stuck. But there was nothing pretty about his life.[34] Men tend to think of bank robbers as dashing, almost heroic figures. Some referred to Floyd as a Robin Hood because of his manners and willingness to throw money around. His life however, like Dillinger's, the lives of Bonnie and Clyde, Ma Barker and kids, and other "Most Wanted", ended in death and heartache for many. It is God who has ordained that the wages of sin is death. Crooks think they are too smart or cool or lucky to pay the price, but what God says goes, and no amount of good looks or good manners will change it. Pretty Boy Floyd's life wasn't pretty because he gave in to the foolish and dissolute dreams of a boy, instead of staying at home and taking care of his family like a real man does.

Only One Rule

Robert E. Lee was commander of the Confederate forces in the Civil War and one of the great generals of all time. I knew a lot about his war years, but almost nothing about his life afterward. The other day I found out. Lee, depressed after the war, would rarely come out of his house to talk to anyone. Some asked entrance, and he always attended to any visitors, but he was stuck in no-man's land for a time, wondering what a 58-year-old retired general could do for a living.

He found out when Washington University in upper-state Virginia, a failing college with only four professors and forty returning students, named him as their new president. Some thought the gesture would be an insult to the old soldier, but he jumped into the job with all his heart and worked tirelessly to make the college stronger and financially stable. He planted bushes and trees, checked on students' test grades, raised money, and sought to mentor the young seventeen-year-old freshmen coming to the school.

You would think that a career soldier would be a strict overseer, but Lee was so kind, gentle, and considerate that some of the younger students found it hard to envision him as a supreme commander of men. One youngster who had cut too many classes and whose grades had dropped had to face Lee and give an explanation. He had made up a whole batch of excuses, and was in the process of sharing them—sickness, left his boots at the cobbler's, accidently overslept—when Lee said, "Stop, sir! One good reason is enough!" The student noticed a twinkle in Lee's eye as he said it. Lee told his faculty he did not believe in forcing boys to do their duty, but in trying to get them to see what was the correct fashion in which they should conduct themselves.

He was rather tolerant of collegiate hi-jinks, telling one student who asked for a copy of the rules, "Young man, we have no printed rules. We have but one rule here, and it is that every student must be a gentleman." [35] Some might disagree, but I think that's quite profound. Which would we rather have, a young person who rigidly follows all written rules but goes wild if there isn't a specific rule forbidding a certain behavior, or a young person who is guided by an inner voice that bids him comport himself in a manner that will bring honor to his name and the name of his family? To ask the question is to answer it. It is a scriptural principle. When asked the greatest commandment Jesus didn't point to any of the ten big ones, or a long list of rules, but to the principle of loving God with everything you are, and loving your neighbor as you love yourself. When you do that you will obey the formal Law, and also the higher law of love that leads you to do far more than the law requires.

Lee lived his own life that way. After the war an insurance company offered to pay him $50,000 a year, an enormous salary in those days, and he wouldn't have to do a thing. The representative said, "We only want your name." Lee's amazing response? Refusing the offer, he said, "Do you not think that if my name is worth fifty thousand dollars a year, I ought to be very careful about taking care of it?" [36] We would all do well to live our lives with honor as this gracious gentleman did, the man who obeyed only one rule.

Overruled!

Operation Overlord was a success, but in its planning it had its tenuous moments. There were big differences of opinion among the high brass in planning for the event. I guess I just assumed everyone planned together in harmony (how naïve could I be?), but there were lots and lots of contrasting opinions on how best to utilize Allied forces. British Air Marshal Trafford Leigh-Mallory (don't you just love those hyphenated British names?) was in charge of the Allied air forces during the Normandy invasion, and his idea was to send Allied planes much further inland to bomb and strafe targets of opportunity during the expected German counterattacks. But Eisenhower, Supreme Allied Commander, overruled him and decided that the planes would bomb and strafe along the coast before the invasion took place. The British didn't want to invade Germany from France anyway. Their idea was what created the Italian invasion and campaign. Eisenhower overruled on that point too. France would be the site of the invasion.

Eisenhower had to broker solutions to disagreements between U.S. Army General George Marshall and British Field Marshal Lord Alanbrooke, and between General George Patton and British Field Marshal Bernard Montgomery (who could imagine George Patton disagreeing with anyone?). Historians say it was Eisenhower's ability to work amicably with others and bring everyone to the table that brought success to what many view as the most important battle of World War II. It didn't hurt that once he had all the facts and opinions, and had thought them through, he was a very decisive leader, and did not hesitate to go ahead with his carefully laid plans.

In January of 1944 Eisenhower was appointed supreme commander. Harry Truman hadn't said it yet, but the "buck stopped" at Eisenhower's desk. Others gave their opinions. There were many discussions and even more disagreements on a host of topics. But in the end Eisenhower had the power to overrule others. It's the only way the operation could have worked. Without a clear chain of command the invasion would never have gotten off the ground. When there are too many voices speaking at once nobody can hear any voice at all. Ike sent the men into combat on June 6th, after calling them off June 5th, and he wrote a letter that said the final decision to pull the trigger on the invasion was his, and his alone.[37]

In a vastly more definitive way the Lord has the ultimate say-so about the direction our lives will take. A rough paraphrase of Proverbs 16:9 is "we can make our plans, but the Lord determines the outcome." It is why, in the final analysis, we need to trust in the Lord with all our hearts and not lean on our own understanding. If we acknowledge Him in all things He will direct our paths, and His ways are always right. (Proverbs 3) He is the highest ranking Commander anyway, and He gets to overrule our often short-sighted decisions. We should be grateful. Imagine if *we* were really in charge.

Refusing to Believe

In late November 1943 American nurses and medical personnel who were on a mission to take care of Allied wounded in Italy during World War II had their plane crash in Albania. They spent more than two harrowing months there hiding from Germans and caught in a crossfire between Albanian factions in a civil war. They suffered tremendously with cold, hunger, and illness, but all survived and were finally rescued and returned to America.

Albania during WWII was one of the poorest countries in the world, and fighting Germans and each other certainly didn't result in having a better quality of life for the native population. They rarely had meat to eat and were often reduced to surviving on onions or cornmeal or maybe some potatoes.

A sidebar to the main story pulls at your heartstrings. An Albanian man named Haki had tired of living in poverty and had worked his way across the Atlantic to America on board a ship. As he sought his fortune he settled in Pennsylvania, working as a cook. He was absolutely amazed at the riches of the New World. He worked hard and saved his money so he could return to Albania for his wife and sons to bring them to this incredible place, so he made the journey home just before the war broke out, and found to his consternation that they wouldn't believe him when he told them of the opportunities, freedom, and luxuries he had encountered. He described hotel rooms with private baths, milk delivered to doorsteps, telephones in each room of the house, and plenty of food for everyone.

They accused him of being mad, and not only would not return to America with him but refused to live with him anymore. He was understandably heartbroken.[38] You, too, have perhaps been heartbroken when you told someone about the glorious truths of the gospel. Forgiveness of sin, all the riches of Christ, abundant provision, joy, peace, direction, and purpose; all are found in the Lord. But some refuse to believe it's that simple. They think there must be a catch, that the promises are not for them.

So they continue to live in spiritual poverty, eking out an existence, barely surviving, instead of responding in faith, taking the journey to see for themselves, and coming to live in the land of promise. Your desire is that they believe Psalm 34:8, to "taste and see that the Lord is good; blessed is the man who hopes in Him..." You have discovered that the promise is true, that the riches of His grace are available, and that those who trust in the Lord are never ashamed. Pray for them as Paul did for the Ephesians, "that you may know what is the hope of His calling, what are the riches of the glory of His inheritance in the saints, and what is the exceeding greatness of His power toward us who believe, according to the working of His mighty power..." (Ephesians 1:18-19) May the Lord grant faith to those who doubt.

Useless

His father was shrewd, talkative, and successful. But the boy was like his mother; withdrawn, extraordinarily quiet and reflective. He wasn't too good at sports and didn't hunt because he couldn't stand the thought of killing things. Small for his age, rather thin, with delicate hands and feet, he was a solitary child. He would not curse as the other boys did; doggone it or confound it were the worst phrases he ever used. Some described him as a bit girlish.

He was an indifferent student, average or below in every subject but math. During recess he hardly ever played with the others, preferring to sit on a stump and watch them instead. His schoolmates though him dull. Even the adults in the village thought so. His father once sent him to bargain for a horse when he was eight. He told the man "Papa says I may offer you twenty dollars for the colt, but if you won't take that to offer you twenty-two and a half, and if you won't take that, to give you twenty-five." The boy certainly didn't understand the art of the deal, and this story circulated widely, shaming the father and the son both.

His one great desire was to escape home someday, because his father was a tanner, and he hated with a passion the stench of death all around the place. His father decided to send him, of all places, to military school. Nobody who knew the boy thought it would work. One neighbor told the father he couldn't believe the congressman who had paved the way for his entrance didn't find another boy with the intellect to *"do credit to the district."* Everything about the young man said he would fail and be sent home in shame. He told his father he wouldn't go, but finally relented, and at age seventeen—117 pounds, five foot one inch tall, fair-skinned, delicate though he was—he made his appearance at the leading military academy in the land.

He piled up demerits for sloppy attire, sloppy habits, and indifferent study, graduating twenty-first in a class of thirty-six. His only strength academically was math, and he thought he would become a math teacher someday. The only other thing he was exceptional at was working with horses. He was the best rider and horse trainer among the cadets. After military school he tried his hand at various things, with little real success. He couldn't help but think of himself as Useless, the nickname he had been given when a boy. [39]

His father thought he was useless. His classmates thought he was useless. The townspeople thought he was useless. Some of his commanding officers were not impressed. But the young man who understood math and horses possessed amazing skills at war. Of all the commanders of the Union forces during the Civil War, one stood out as the most responsible for victory, and thus for the preservation of the United States. "Useless" Grant won the war for the North, accepted Lee's surrender at Appomattox, and eventually became the 18th President of the United States. And nobody saw it coming. They thought he was useless. Be careful about assuming that someone else is useless. God may have very great uses for them after all.

Chapter Four—
Lessons From War

The last chapter was on lessons from history, and a few reflections mention incidents that occurred in wartime. Nothing captures the human imagination like war. Soldiers in uniform, rigid discipline, heroic deeds, danger and intrigue and death; war has it all. Supposedly Robert E. Lee once said, "It is a good thing war is so terrible, otherwise we would grow too fond of it." [40] This statement is certainly true enough, although some might disagree with it, but one thing nobody can deny is that whether fond of war or not, we are all captivated by it. Nothing causes more people to seek God—to drop to their knees in prayer, and to plead with God—like war. War disrupts families, brings suffering and pain and death, and leaves lasting scars. There are lessons we learn in it that are deep and abiding. War is terrible, but until all men surrender to the rule of the Prince of Peace in their lives, war is inevitable. Without Christ men seem unable to do anything except demonize the "other." Only in Christ can the other become a brother.

A Dumb Move

After the Normandy invasion of WWII, men who were injured were transported back to England for surgery and recovery. Many of the men, after lengthy stays in the hospital, were declared fit for service again.

It was at that point that two different philosophies became evident. For the Airborne divisions the policy was for men who recovered to be returned to their original company, where the commanding officers were the same and many of the faces were familiar. It eased the transition for the men returning to action. They were back among friends for whom they would give their lives. In a real sense it was like going home again.

The army infantry had a different policy altogether. When men were in the kind of shape needed to fight, they were sent wherever they were needed. For an administrator this made sense. The man was considered a "replacement part", capable of fitting into the war machine wherever there was a lack of personnel. The problems with this philosophy were numerous, however. The man, a combat Veteran, was sent to a unit with which he was unfamiliar. The routines, the officers, the men were all strangers to him. And without exception those men who suffered this fate had a hard time adjusting. War is hard enough without removing everything familiar from the experience. The men almost felt like they were back at boot camp, rookies in the army.

To a man the infantry personnel felt this move was "one of the dumbest things the Army did."[41] Soldiers need routine, and they need camaraderie. It's hard enough to get used to mortar rounds landing near your foxhole without trying to get used to a brand-new foxhole buddy to share the misery with.

A Long Eternity

The French village of La Roche-Guyon was occupied by German forces in June 1944. The most celebrated German general of the war was billeted there; Erwin Rommel, the "Desert Fox", the man who Hitler had designated commander of German forces repelling the anticipated Allied invasion. The Allies were coming, no doubt about that. They had been building up supplies, men, and materiel for months in preparation for their push to retake France and fight their way into Germany to hasten the war's end, but where would they strike, and when? That was the million-dollar question for which the Germans had no answer.

Characteristically Rommel took the assignment with competence and proficiency, stiffening German lines and dramatically increasing beach obstacles, mines, and firepower along the coast. The trouble was it was a long coast to defend, 800 miles of coast to be exact. The Allies had expertly given false signals as to the site of the invasion. So the Germans, aware that an invasion was imminent, prepared to receive it. Rommel knew this battle of the ages would be the decisive one of the war—and unless the Germans could repel the invaders at the sea's edge they would be undone—so he prepared for what he knew would be "the longest day."

As we know from history, D-Day was a bloodbath, especially on Omaha beach, but what many don't know is that it could have been *much* worse. To a large degree and despite arduous preparations for the day, the Germans were caught napping. Sunday, June 4th, 1944, less than 48 hours before the greatest invasion of all time, Rommel decided to take a brief leave. He had worked tirelessly for so long, he was very weary, but he also wanted to visit personally with Hitler to get clearance for plans he had to improve the German defenses. Besides, his wife Lucie's birthday was two days away, and he had bought her a new set of shoes he wanted to deliver in person. He hadn't been home in months, and he believed the invasion wouldn't occur for several weeks. The timing of his trip couldn't have been better...for the Allies.

In addition to Rommel's absence on the dramatic day, the weather was so bad June 5th that the Germans couldn't believe an operation of this magnitude would be attempted by the Allies. They had studied other Allied invasions, such as in North Africa, and they were convinced the Allies would never attack unless the weather was perfect; and it certainly was far from that. Surely they would wait for better conditions. Antiaircraft personnel were ordered to stand down, Rommel's chief of staff, General Hans Spiedel, planned a dinner party for the night of June 5th, while Major Friedrich Hayn made arrangements for another party for the corps commander, General Erich Marcks. Many senior members of German defenses at Normandy left the evening of June 5th to conduct a map exercise dealing with a theoretical invasion of the Normandy coast, little knowing that by that time the real invasion of that coast was already underway. The Luftwaffe had inexplicably decided to transfer its last remaining fighter squadrons in France far from the Normandy beaches. Hitler himself was no better prepared for the invasion. He was in his Berchtesgaden retreat in Bavaria with his mistress Eva Braun, along with many high-ranking officers.

Then German intelligence got the second coded message they had been anticipating and realized that the invasion was indeed on. They alerted General Von Rundstedt and tried to get word to Rommel, who was breakfasting with Lucie. General Marcks was still at his birthday party when the phone rang, alerting him to paratroopers landing in Normandy, but the messages he sent out got garbled in a communications snafu, and precious response time was wasted. Rundstedt still believed the Normandy assault was a "diversionary attack" and not the real invasion. A call came to Alfred Jodl, Hitler's chief of staff, but Jodl decided not to wake the Fuhrer because he might fly into one of his legendary tantrums and make a foolish, emotional decision. So the long and the short of it was that the Germans, after all their preparations, were unready for the greatest day of war planet earth has ever known. [42]

There is coming another day too, a day for which we all must prepare. This time it won't be the sight of thousands of Allied ships and tens of thousands of troops on the horizon, but the sight of the King of kings making His appearance. It is a day we anticipate, we know will come, but when? That is the burning question. It has been "delayed" so long that for many this seems a good time to go on leave or have a party. Surely it won't be today! But eternity is long, don't be wrong. The day will come, and it is nearer now than before. When He comes to earth again, will He find us ready to meet Him, or, as in the days of Noah, will we be eating and drinking and going about our regular lives, unaware until it's too late that the long-anticipated day of judgment, a day that brings in an even longer eternity, is finally here?

A Normal Situation

Captain Dick Winters led his men into the Belgian town of Uden in the fall of 1944. He and a Captain Dixon climbed up into the local church belfry to try and find the Germans they had expected to encounter earlier. They found them alright. They saw German tanks cutting the road behind their previous position, and spotted a German patrol coming towards them from the opposite direction. Winters gathered his platoon and calmly told them, "Men, there's nothing to get excited about. The situation is normal; *we are surrounded.*"[43]

Seems like a funny thing to be calm about. But Winters, a veteran of the Normandy invasion and several other battles over the past days, was unfazed. We as Christians in postmodern America are surrounded in a sense, surrounded by a culture that has gone off its collective rocker, surrounded by a culture that no longer values the things we hold dearest.

But it's normal. When has true biblical Christianity not been surrounded by a culture that did not understand or appreciate it? Neither the Jews nor the Romans understood the first group of believers. The Romans called them atheists because they did not believe in the pantheon of Roman gods or the divinity of the Emperor. England did not appreciate or approve of the Puritans, so they fled to America. The Puritans did not appreciate or approve of Roger Williams and his Baptist doctrine, so he fled to Rhode Island. True Christians have been a minority in almost all the places where God puts them, and the secular culture around them can't figure them out. Many so-called "intellectuals" have railed against Christian teachings for decades here in America, and they have done a good job of producing a couple of generations of wild-eyed acolytes that despise the Christian faith and want to usher in their own secular utopia which includes torching stores, setting up their own country in downtown Seattle, first known as CHAZ (Capitol Hill Autonomous Zone), then as CHOP (Capitol Hill Organized Protest). These radicals, who rail against traditional Christian values, want to defund police, continue to cause chaos throughout the country, and bring in a Marxist agenda, and they have the left-wing media and much of Wall Street on their side.

So Christians are surrounded by voices that seek to drown them out. What to do? Well, Captain Winters decided when he was surrounded there was only one thing to do: attack! He organized the attack, hit the German patrol hard, and drove it back. The Germans were so surprised by the aggressiveness of the Americans that they pulled out, thinking the Allied force was much larger than they at first had considered.

That's a pretty good strategy for believers too. In these days of social media we have excellent opportunities to voice our collective opinion, to be aggressive in championing scriptural truths to a larger culture. The last thing we want to do is to retreat within our enclaves and stay quiet. The enemy will not go away if we employ that strategy. Instead we are to submit to God and resist the devil. Resistance doesn't just mean standing against, it means going on the attack. It may be normal for us to be surrounded, but as God's army we must never surrender or retreat when we are in the right.

Army of Resistance

The young colonel was unaccustomed to war, and it showed. He built a place of defense on ground that was too low and exposed, and open to the elements. Then he tried to hold his "fort" despite the fact that there was no compelling reason to do so. It resulted in the loss of many of his men. Later, as a general, he continued to make mistakes. There were times he should have attacked but hesitated; other times where he attacked unwisely. One of his major adversaries outfoxed him on several important occasions, and his troops were defeated badly. In one battle he split up his forces when he should have kept them together, and it resulted in a disaster that could have ended the war right there except for what he believed was God's intervention. He kept being obsessed with taking a particular city that actually did not need to be taken in order for his army to have success. Officers within his own ranks said he was "dithering and indecisive." [44]

Yet despite these mistakes, and indeed because of them, he learned. He learned that there is nothing like victory to improve men's morale, and that with an inferior force ill-equipped for battle at times, it was unwise to press the attack against a superior foe. What he learned most of all was that winning battles and holding ground was not as critical as holding his army together and continuing the fight. In a letter to one of his backers, he stated "The possession of our towns, while we have an army in the field, will avail [the enemy] little...It is our arms, not defenseless towns, they have to subdue." [45] As long as he and the army didn't surrender, as long as they didn't capitulate, as long as they existed and were willing to continue the struggle, their enemy could never declare final victory. So the general turned his attention to encouraging enlistments and discouraging desertions. Finally, after years of battle and struggles to keep his army together, his ragtag bunch claimed victory over the most powerful force on earth, and a new nation was born.

George Washington is considered one of the most important leaders in world history, but it's not because of his incredible battle strategies. Despite his own unquestioned personal courage and integrity, some of his plans were questionable at best, and his best plans often involved withdrawal of troops and just surviving to fight another day, a day where the odds were more in his favor. England eventually got tired of spending blood and treasure in a far-off war fighting an elusive enemy, and they gave it up. The American people were so grateful for Washington's leadership that they made him the president of the Constitutional Convention and eventually of the United States.

We are reminded of James 4:7. "Therefore submit to God. Resist the devil and he will flee from you." Even though we know that "greater is He that is in us than he that is in the world" (I John 4:4), we certainly sometimes feel that we are oppressed by a more powerful foe than we can conquer, overwhelmed by the assaults brought into our lives. And yet, like Washington, we can learn this valuable lesson: continual resistance to enemy attack ends up encouraging us and discouraging him. And in the end he will flee, as long as we continue to fight. Don't desert the cause. Keep resisting and watch your enemy give up and quit the field of battle.

Currahee

Currahee is a Cherokee word that means *"stand alone."* There is a mountain right next to Camp Toccoa in Georgia called Currahee Mountain, and during WWII the men of Easy Company, 506th parachute regiment, became very familiar with it. They had to run to its top many times, sometimes multiple times a day, "Three miles up, and three miles down." Their physical conditioning became so strong that when they later went to Ft. Benning for parachute school they were allowed to skip phase A, which was physical conditioning, because the drill sergeants there couldn't keep up with them. Army airborne training was rigorous, to say the least.

Currahee became the battle-cry and motto of Easy Company. In the paratroops you might find yourself standing alone or standing with only a few buddies, because by its nature parachuting in the dark behind enemy lines tends to separate men from one another.

These elite troops were the first in action during the momentous D-Day invasion of June 1944, dropped in the middle of the night behind German lines. To their credit, small bands of men began to carry out their mission, despite being separated and missing their drop zones. Clusters of soldiers worked hard to fulfill their duties, and slowly they began to run into other groups doing the same. [46]

How we in the body of Christ must have this motto as well. We are commanded to not forsake assembling, because we need to be encouraged by one another. But then, due to circumstances we often cannot control, we sometimes find ourselves divided into smaller groups, and we must not allow that to distract us from the work we can do. Building God's kingdom is a monumental task, and it requires all of us to do our part, whether we are joined by huge groups to encourage us or not. Then when we have opportunity to join up with others of like faith, we can work together in a more concentrated way to achieve the Lord's objectives.

Easy Company used Currahee as a rallying cry, and they defined it thusly: stand alone—together! It seems impossible. How can you stand alone if you are not by yourself? Well, obviously we as believers must band together to stand with each other against the prevailing cultural insanity rampant in our country today. Lone Ranger Christianity is not biblical. We must find others—even if it is only a few— others we can work with to increase God's kingdom where we are. God give us strength to stand alone against the prevailing lies of our culture, and give us wisdom to do our standing alone together with others who love the Lord.

Don't Be Late

The Colonel called for a regimental parade and addressed the men. "You are members of one of the finest regiments in the United States Army, and consequently in the world. Much of your training has been completed, and you have won your wings. I am sending each of you home on a 10-day furlough. Remember that certain things are expected of you. You are to live by the creed of the elite, to let that creed govern your life. Stay out of jail; honor your unit and your name and your country. Walk and talk with pride and military bearing; take care of your personal appearance. Don't forget to be back on base in good time. *After the time runs out, you are considered AWOL.*"

The men were released to their own recognizance after the speech, and they headed to the bus and train stations to go north, south, east, or west and enjoy home-cooked meals, visits with moms and dads and siblings and girlfriends, and recreations that were not part of camp life. They were excited, boisterous, confident, and justifiably proud of their achievements.

But some of them had so much fun at home that they failed to return to base in time. For some it was a missed train departure while they made their long goodbyes. Some couldn't find a cab at the right time, or got in a traffic jam, or had a delay at the bus station. Certainly there were unforeseen obstacles that kept them from getting back across the country on time. How could you blame them if they were a bit late returning to base?

Nevertheless, the day after their return the Colonel called them again to parade, this time in dress uniform. A lieutenant solemnly read the name of a private, who was ushered forward by two sergeants carrying machine guns as a drummer tapped a dreary march, and then the Colonel ceremoniously tore off the patch from the private's arm, took the precious wings off his chest, removed the parachute patch from his hat, and threw them on the ground. The private was being drummed out of the paratroopers and consigned to the infantry. The last humiliation came as the young man had to take off the special boots only paratroopers were permitted to wear, and return to wearing pants "straight legs", no longer allowed to stuff pants into the boots. He was no longer elite. [47]

It is a great responsibility to belong to an elite group. To be associated with them is an honor, but it requires integrity and care to uphold their name. A Christian is a "little Christ", and thus bears the Name of the greatest One of all. A Christian is part of an elite group of warriors, spiritual warriors who fight spiritual battles. Let us carry His name with joy and sobriety. It is a high honor. And let us never be late in exhibiting Him as Lord of our lives.

Know the Opposing Commander

There is a maxim in war that a great general does not focus as much on the number and placement of opposing troops or their armament, but rather primarily on something beyond. What could be *beyond* these crucial factors when going into battle? The great general contemplates his opposing number—the general on the other side—as his first consideration.

This is certainly what George Patton did in North Africa when his tanks faced those of Erwin Rommel. Some historians claim Rommel, the Desert Fox, was the greatest general of all time, and his tank commanders and armament were top flight, considered unbeatable by many observers. When Patton took over 2nd Army Tank Corps it was full of undisciplined officers and men who had suffered setbacks that left them dispirited and lacking in confidence for future battles. Patton had ten days to prepare his men for the fateful battle of El Guettar. He went into his raging bull mode, kicked some officers in the backside, and forced his men to prepare for the fight of their lives.

But he also had a secret. He had studied Rommel like nobody else had studied him. And Rommel actually made it easier for him—he had written a book about tank tactics. Amazingly, Patton's forces won the battle decisively because Patton anticipated Rommel's moves, and Patton famously shouted across the desert, *"Rommel, I read your book!"*[48]

The opposing leader for Christians is Satan. He has a playbook that contains strategies he always uses when fighting believers. He hasn't personally written a book, but The Book tells us about it. 2nd Corinthians 2:10-11 reminds us that we are not ignorant of his schemes. Read the Bible all the way through and notice Satan using the same tactics over and over again…

*Lies—John 8:44

*Discouragement—Joshua 1

*Accusation—Revelation 12:10

*Intimidation—I Peter 5:8

*Fear—II Timothy 1:7

*False promises—Genesis 3

*Deception—convincing Judas that betraying Jesus was a good idea, for example

The devil has used the same playbook for all human history to attack and ruin lives. We need to read the book and know who opposes us. That, more than any other thing, will bring us victory. Sun Tzu was an ancient military strategist who wrote a book called *The Art of War*. His insights are helpful here...

"*If you know the enemy and know yourself, you need not fear the result of a hundred battles. If you know yourself but not the enemy, for every victory gained you will also suffer a defeat. If you know neither the enemy nor yourself, you will succumb in every battle.*"[49] Keep these truths in mind when battling our ancient foe.

Practice Needed

The soldiers had already proven that they could fight well at night. They showed that during the Normandy invasion as they were dropped behind German lines and successfully achieved their objectives. Afterward they were shipped to England to rest and prepare for their next assignment.

While there they did further training at night, jumping onto English soil to work on various components of communication and tactics and improve their ability to achieve new objectives. What was interesting was that they were in competition with other units during these exercises. They won each head-to-head matchup easily. Why were they so good at night operations?

Because they trained in parachute school under Captain Herbert Sobel, a man universally despised by his men. The joke going around the unit was "Who will kill Sobel when his back is turned during battle?" The men weren't kidding. Sobel belittled men, took revenge on soldiers he didn't like, often irritated his men for no good reason, and was something of a disaster in leading men on the battlefield. But he demanded the best of the men when it came to training, and he demanded that they do a lot of their training in the dark, because the operation required them to jump at night and begin their attacks at night.

The men feared Sobel would lead them to disaster when the real fighting started, and to their great relief he was removed as company commander before Operation Overlord. But they found when the fighting started, and they were reminded later when their training continued, that they were the best night fighters in the world. And they were that good in large part because of a hated commanding officer who deserved the resentment of his troops. He was not a magnanimous or self-sacrificing man, and he did not understand his men at all. But he did do them a real favor by training them so hard, and he undoubtedly saved many lives when they faced Germans who were trying to kill them. [50]

God's training regimen is sometimes hard. We chaff at the pressure He puts on us to grow up and become disciplined. Hebrews 12 says nobody enjoys the discipline while it's happening, but then later that same discipline produces the peaceable fruit of righteousness to those who have been trained by it. Paul told us in I Corinthians 9 that he trained spiritually in a serious way, because he didn't want to preach to others and then be disqualified. Training for war is a serious matter. We should not grumble when the Lord requires much discipline from us. He—unlike Captain Sobel—does understand us, care about us, and sacrifice for us. Like Sobel, He knows that when the real shooting starts we need to have gone over our assignment many times so we can do it... even in the dark.

The Double

In late spring 1944 the phone rang at M.E. Clifton James' desk. Like all good Englishmen, James was doing his best to help the war effort against Nazi Germany, serving in the Royal Army Pay Corps office. Unbelievably, it was actor (and Colonel) David Niven on the phone with a question. "Would you like to help us make some Army films?" James, an actor himself, jumped at the chance, and soon found himself in London. Niven met him, then left him with a Colonel Lester, who told James the real reason he had been called to London. "I am a member of

MI 5, Army intelligence, and we want you to pose as General Bernard Montgomery's double in a high stakes game of disinformation we hope will keep the Germans guessing on our plans for the invasion of France."

James was initially intimidated with the assignment, but willing to do his best. Bearing an uncanny resemblance to "Monty", James began an intense program of study, studying newspaper photographs and watching newsreels of the famous general, drilled by Lester on hundreds of details of the impersonation. James eventually spent several days on Monty's staff where he could study him close at hand. He learned Monty was a strict non-smoker, a teetotaler, and a fanatic about physical fitness. At meals the general rarely spoke of war at all in those unguarded moments. James noted the way Monty saluted his men, how he ate, his habit of throwing out one hand in emphasis when he wanted to make a point, and most importantly, the confidence the man showed, the swagger and the way he strutted about when inspecting troops.

James was finally given a private interview with the acclaimed man. James listened carefully to the incisive, high-pitched voice and the way he chose his words. He knew he would have to practice much to pull off the ruse. His assignment was to go to Gibraltar posing as Monty, then to North Africa as well to be seen by Nazi spies. He was to talk of the purely fictional attack of the Allies on southern France originating in North Africa in hopes the Germans would divert manpower there and draw troops and resources away from the actual D-Day site: Normandy.

The trickery worked better than the English could have hoped. The Germans were convinced that James was Monty, and that an attack would be made from North Africa. They didn't find out their mistake until June 6, 1944.[51]

Fascinating story, but what does that have to do with us? Well, we have received a call from the High Command as well, a call to do our best to mimic a renowned Man. Peter said Jesus left us an example and that we should "follow in His steps." (I Peter 2:21) John told us that whoever abides in Him should walk as He walked. (I John 2:6) It's an intimidating command for us. How in the world do we act like the

Lord? Obviously, we can't do it perfectly. There is only one sinless Christ. But we can do what Clifton James did...*study*. We can try to get to know our Lord so well that walking in His steps becomes more natural to us. And we can "interview" Him often, watch Him carefully, pick up expressions of His character. Our name? *Christian*, meaning "little Christ." May the world see Him when we walk as His double.

The Faith of a Child

His nickname was Skinny. Promoted to sergeant, he had survived front line duty with the most famous company of soldiers in World War II, Easy Company of the 101st Airborne Division. The war was winding down, and he was part of the mop-up crew that got to see the destruction of Hitler's "Eagles Nest". Tens of thousands of German soldiers were surrendering by the day.

But there were a few of the German officers that knew if they surrendered they would be tried for war crimes and executed, so they stayed in the hills hoping to escape capture. Sergeant Skinny Sisk, along with a few others, was given orders to track one of them down and shoot him.

They found the German officer, who ran off. Skinny took aim with his M1 rifle and killed him with one shot. It wasn't the first German Skinny had killed. It was war, after all, kill or be killed, every man for himself.

They say war is hell, but it's not just hell for those who lose. It's also hard on those who win and return home. Few of those who killed others, even in war, can forget it and escape the memories. Skinny couldn't. Here is his own testimony that he sent to Major Dick Winters in 1991...

"My career after the war was trying to drink away the truckload of Krauts that I stopped in Holland and the die-hard Nazi that I went up into the Bavarian Alps and killed. Old Moe Alley made a statement that all the killings that I did was going to jump into the bed with me one of these days and they sure did. I had a lot of flashbacks after the war and I started drinking."

Poor soldier. Placed in an incredibly stressful situation as a young man, he did his duty as he saw it and then couldn't escape the doing of his duty. Many returning soldiers fall into deep depression, try to cover the pain with drugs or alcohol, and many end up taking their own lives. Thankfully that didn't happen to Skinny. Let him tell you why...

"...my little sister's daughter, four-years-old, came into my bedroom. I was too unbearable to the rest of the family, either hung over or drunk. She told me that Jesus loved me and she loved me and if I would repent God would forgive me for all the men I kept trying to kill all over again. That little girl got to me. I put her out of my room, told her to go to her Mommy. There and then I bowed my head on my Mother's feather bed and repented and God forgave me for the war and all the other bad things I had done down through the years. I was ordained in the latter part of 1949 into the ministry...the Lord willing and Jesus tarries I hope to see you all at the next reunion." [52]

There is the power of the Gospel, the power of forgiveness found at the Cross, the power of the Holy Spirit to bring conviction to a man everyone had given up hope of ever reaching. There also is the power of the words of an innocent child, who in simple faith in her Lord and in her uncle shared the truth that sets souls free.

Too Big a Hurry

In May 1941 Nazi Germany sent the largest battleship ever produced into the fight against the Allies. This heavily armored "unsinkable" ship was nearly three football fields in length and had eight 15 inch guns that could hurl over 15,000 pounds of steel at her enemies with every firing. Each gun had enough power to hurl a small car 22 miles. That's some firepower! This ship could move 35 miles per hour, making her one of the fastest ships afloat as well as the most powerful. 2200 German sailors were proud to be setting out on the maiden voyage of the most fearsome ship ever manufactured. It was fast, powerful, and state-of-the-art.

Chapter Four—Lessons From War

But the *Bismarck* never came home, and over 2000 of those men met a watery grave within just a few days. Why? First, the *Bismarck* left secretly and sailed to a fiord in German-occupied Norway. While making final preparations to sail into the north Atlantic and wreak havoc on Allied shipping, the Bismarck was spotted and photographed by a British Spitfire. The *Bismarck's* voyage was a secret no more. The Germans made a crucial mistake at this point. Anxious to get out into water where it could maneuver, the captain failed to refill the ship's fuel supply. Other "hurries", these in *Bismarck's* construction, now plagued her. The Germans had new technologies for every part of the ship except her antiaircraft guns. The *Bismarck's* guns were outdated and could not fire in an effective way. In addition, on May 23, 1941, the British ships *Norfolk* and *Suffolk* spotted the *Bismarck* and gave chase through the Denmark Strait. For the first time, the *Bismarck* fired her big guns, but hurt only herself in the process, because her main radar antenna had been hastily installed and was knocked out of commission by the violent recoil caused by the huge cannons.

With the *Suffolk* and *Norfolk* on her heels, *Bismarck* fled. British ships *Prince of Wales* and *Hood* were converging from the southeast to intercept her and join in the fight. The *Hood* was the British navy's flagship, its own "unsinkable" titan which had never lost a battle. At 5:35 a.m. on May 24th the ships saw each other, but the sailors aboard *Bismarck* were cocky, convinced that nothing could defeat them. At first this faith was justified, for one of their shells hit *Hood* in its magazine, and the entire ship with its 1400 member crew was destroyed. But a 14-inch shell from *Prince of Wales* blew through *Bismarck's* bow, rupturing a fuel line. Seawater poured in, and a thousand tons of much needed fuel was rendered useless. *Bismarck* could now no longer move so quickly, and she headed for German-occupied France for repairs, shadowed by the British ships, who maintained radar contact with her.

British Swordfish planes converged on the German ship, now nearly out of fuel. Because *Bismarck* was rushed into service and her crew had not practiced sufficiently, her antiquated antiaircraft guns, incredibly, did not hit one British plane. A torpedo fired by one British aircraft hit *Bismarck* in the rudder, and she could no longer navigate. The *Bismarck*, crippled, was doomed. She could no longer maneuver, and as British ships surrounded her, she absorbed shell after shell until she sank beneath the waves to rise no more. [53]

Don't get in too big a hurry! The Germans rushed the *Bismarck* to war before she or her crew were ready. They hurriedly installed her radar antenna which led to its failure. They hurriedly installed inadequate antiaircraft guns, manned by inadequately trained gunners. She left Norway hurriedly, failing to refuel. In life, make sure you are ready when you sail. They say that haste makes waste. It also can cost you in life's battles.

Chapter Five—
Motivation

So far we've learned from many lives. Their stories are instructive. Each person was motivated by some inner or external force to behave as they did. Teaching and preaching put you in the people business, and it is part of your job description to instruct, inspire, and motivate those under your care. Motivation is that drive that causes you to get up, suit up, and play in the game of life. There are as many motivators as there are people I would imagine, and I have tried over the years to find quotes and principles that stir people's blood so they will *move* in a direction that means a better life for them. Like Zig Ziglar once said, "If you aim at nothing, you'll hit it every time!"[54] I have always hoped to inspire those around me to aim for something worthy, and pursue it with all their strength. As a coach, a teacher, a mentor, a youth pastor, and a pastor I have searched for keys to unlock the inner drives within others so that they will pursue the things in life that make it worthwhile and satisfying.

Aim For the Center of the Bull's-Eye

At the time this receiver retired from professional football he was widely viewed as the greatest receiver in NFL history. There is an interesting story behind his success. He played college football for SMU in the 1950's, and in a critical game against the University of Texas he fumbled twice, both times with his team in critical field position. SMU barely lost the game, and went on to lose the conference championship by a half game. He obviously felt terrible about the loss, and took personal responsibility for it.

He became obsessed with catching and holding on to the football. In a 13-year professional career with the Baltimore Colts, being the favorite target of his quarterback, absorbing many hits during each game, he fumbled exactly *once*...and he says the ref made a mistake on that call! An old veteran receiver once told him to "watch the ball into your hands." It made him one of the greatest football players of his generation.[55]

Raymond Berry became a motivational speaker after his hall-of-fame playing days were over. His mantra for his audiences was "Don't aim for the bull's-eye; aim for *center* of the bull's-eye!"[56] In other words, work at doing things the right way, and you'll never be sorry.

By the way, his quarterback for most of those pass completions? Another hall-of-famer, Johnny Unitas.

By Littles

Abraham Lincoln grew from a rough country bumpkin into the most admired president in U.S. history. His father, Thomas, was an uneducated man and didn't want Abe filled with too much book learning, preferring that he spend time on the farm helping Thomas make ends meet. For that reason, Abraham, who loved school, was shortchanged when it came to formal schooling. His times at school were too infrequent and short-lived, and he called it learning "by littles." [57]

As a Sunday school teacher, youth leader, and pastor over the years I have been blessed by getting to teach some remarkably quick students, students who could absorb big quantities of information (many of them my own children). It's fun as a teacher to have students who could process rapidly and with understanding. But there have been times I have in my classes or congregations students (of all ages) who aren't able or willing to "come to school" regularly. At that point we have to start again at the basics. The other day in Sunday school two of the students who came were not regulars, and had a very cursory knowledge of the Bible, so we reviewed how to find verses in Scripture, what was the first book of the Bible, what were the first few books of the New Testament, and so forth. We told using pictures and leading questions the story of Joseph (the class age ranged from 5 to 11-years-old).

It is hard to be patient as a teacher. I want the kids to learn, learn it fast, and grow mature in their understanding of God's Word. There is so much to talk about, so much to learn. But especially for those children who come infrequently, their learning is by littles. I have always longed for students (again, of all ages) who are hungry to learn and want to grow in their understanding of truth. Abraham Lincoln was such a person. He of course was gifted with an outstanding intellect even though born in poverty, but he also had an insatiable yearning to KNOW. He would read the few books around him so many times he virtually memorized them, and he developed a life-long love affair with the Bible. His greatest speeches used scriptural references and allusions, and you can hear the cadence of King James English in them. I hope all parents and adults will develop that appetite for knowing the best of books. When some former Maryland slaves gifted Lincoln a copy of the holy book in 1864, he replied "In regard to this great book, it is the best gift God has ever given to man. All the good from the Savior of the world is communicated to us through this Book." [58]

May the day come when adults will lead children to study and know God's truth. Far too many fail to attend Sunday school or other weekly study sessions, and fail as well to study on their own. When a person gets serious about knowing, the learning accelerates, and instead of learning by littles, they, as Lincoln did, begin to learn "by *lots*."

Chazzek Yourself

In I Samuel 30 David found himself in a pickle. He and his men returned home to find their city burned and their families kidnapped by raiders. For David it went from bad to worse, for his men talked of stoning him (talk about getting thrown under the bus!). But verse 6 says that David strengthened himself in the Lord his God. The Hebrew word for strengthen there is "chazzek", pronounced "hazzock". There are at least 12 profound meanings of this word. To chazzek is to...

1) *"make strong"*. The book of Hebrews mentions that by faith those that were weak became strong. We become strong in faith by *exercise*, by *practice*. This requires discipline, discipline which the Lord requires of us but richly rewards when we engage in it.

2) *"encourage"*, to *"root for or cheer for."* It's the picture of the runner moving around the track or along the cross country path, with people yelling for them, telling them how well they are doing, pulling for them. Encouragement comes from Latin, where the middle part "cour" comes from the same root as cardio, so to encourage means to "give heart". When you want to give up, you instead give heart. If you've seen "Overcomer" by the Kendrick brothers, Alex plays a basketball coach that is forced to coach cross country, something he doesn't even consider a sport. He is challenged to run 3 miles. As he does so he talks to himself, cheering for himself. "Don't die, don't die, don't die."

3) *"repair"*. Anybody got a tractor or mower or car? Does it ever have to be repaired? Do parts ever wear out? Does the constant grind on the machine take a toll? It is the same in the Christian life. Life is often a grind, and our souls need repairing. Here David repaired himself "in the Lord." His soul needed healing, so he went to the place of healing in God. Scripture says "there is a balm in Gilead", and we need to apply that balm today.

4) *"fortify"*, like a city broken into whose walls have been damaged or removed. We must rebuild those walls of righteousness, in our own lives first, and then in our families and ultimately in our nation. Think of every time you give in to discouragement you are taking bricks out of the protective wall against Satan, and every time you encourage yourself in the Lord you are building

that wall. It does something for your spirit when you feel like a wall-builder.
5) *"be obstinate."* Obstinate has both a bad and good connotation. We are never to be obstinate with God or with people trying to help us, instead we are to have soft and pliable hearts for the Lord to plant His seed; but we are to be obstinate with regard to sin and evil. We are to be obstinate in faith, in hope. We are to be "stubborn" in our righteousness. "No, I will not cave in to discouragement or despair; I will trust in God no matter what." God told Ezekiel "make your face like flint" because God was sending him to a people who did not want to hear his message and he was going to get pushback. Situations and people are going to push back when you dedicate yourself to following God. Be prepared for it. Be obstinate. Stubbornly cling to God.

In the next blog we'll look at seven other meanings of strengthening ourselves in God.

Chazzek Yourself Part II

One of the crucial skills in the Christian life is to learn to encourage yourself in the Lord. David strengthened himself in God, and we are to do the same. Here are other meanings of the Hebrew word used in I Samuel 30:6. To "chazzek" (strengthen) ourselves means to...
1) *"continue."* The long-distance runner talks to himself thru the race, saying "don't give up, head for that marker, then the next. One foot in front of the other, one step at a time, don't quit, don't quit, don't quit." When we feel we can't continue we must find in the Lord the strength to keep going. My brother as a coach is a big believer in running track to prepare for other sports. Not only does it make you physically faster, but more important it makes you *mentally tougher.* "I can't do this training

regimen you are requiring of me." "Sure you can, and the sooner you see that the sooner you get the benefits in every area of life."

2) *"lean on."* David is giving himself something (or Someone) to lean on during this crisis. We often mess up, and want to quit in bitterness and discouragement. But we have someone to lean on so we can finish the race. Remember the amazing story of Derek Redmond, a British sprinter who had qualified for the semifinal round of the 400 m dash in the Barcelona Olympics? He had the fastest time in his preliminary round and was looking strong in the semis, when his hamstring tore. In agony, instead of crumpling to the ground, he heroically attempted to finish the race. The crowd, hurting for him and cheering him on, watched in awe as an older man ran out onto the track and finished the race with Derek's arm around his shoulder. It was Derek's father Jim. Derek leaned on his father, and both of them, tears in their eyes, finished the race. We must lean on our Father to help us when we are torn and unable to finish alone.

3) *"recover."* Interestingly, Derek Redmond became a motivational speaker. He took the heartbreaking difficulty in those Olympic games and recovered to help others. You think your trials and failures make you unqualified to speak to others? No, they qualify you. You have a message to give to others. Derek didn't win an Olympic medal in 1992. That was his goal. It would have given him a platform to speak into the lives of others. Instead he got another platform, one even better. He could speak to failure, to difficulty, to overcoming odds.

4) *"withstand."* Ever feel overwhelmed, like if one more problem gets piled on top of you, you'll break? Being a husband, a father, a mother, is being under pressure. You are under pressure to provide, to be wise, to have it all together, to be tough, but also tender. As the apostle Paul said of the Christian life, "who is adequate for these things?" But he gives us the immediate answer to his question: "but our adequacy is of God." We can withstand

the pressures and be molded into God's image by the pressures if we will continually bring ourselves back to the Lord.

5) ***"grow mighty."*** To be mighty is to be fearsome, tough, impressively strong, *manly*. As Arnold Schwarzenegger says, *not a girly man*. Interesting that in the definition of mighty is the idea of a man standing up to the enemies of his life and conquering them. The Lord said to Cain, "sin lies at the door. And its desire is for you, but you must master it, rule over it." (Genesis 4) God says the same thing to everyone. Now we know we can only be mighty in the Lord, but we *can* be mighty. To strengthen yourself in the Lord means to be tough with sin, to conquer it.

6) ***"be valiant."*** To be valiant is to be fearless, brave, *plucky*. It means to show "grit." We admire grit. When John Wayne, playing Rooster Cogburn, takes those reins in his teeth and starts his horse toward the four bad guys, it makes one of the iconic images in movie history. Where is our grit against giving up? By ourselves we are not a hero, but in God we can rise up to the challenge.

7) Lastly chazzek means ***"to prevail."*** To prevail is to finish the race, to complete the task, to get to the end. David went to the end of his life loving God. And David isn't the only bible hero to prevail. You know Joseph strengthened himself a bunch of times during the discouragements he faced. Joshua and Caleb aged 40 years walking in the wilderness, but returned ready to fight. They prevailed. Moses himself could have quit, I'm sure was tempted to quit, but he prevailed to become a spiritual giant. Daniel prevailed when taken to Babylon. Peter prevailed even though he denied Christ. He rebounded to become the leader of the early church. Paul prevailed over an amazing litany of problems and pressures and trials. All these saints strengthened themselves. They often had nobody else to encourage them, but they encouraged themselves in the Lord their God. We must learn to do the same!

Explode Where You Are

Alfred Nobel, a Swedish chemist and engineer, invented dynamite in 1866 (and yes, he made money on the deal and began funding for the Nobel Prizes). Since 1866 dynamite has had many purposes. Purveyors of warfare immediately recognized that the explosive power of dynamite could stop troop movements, disable and kill enemy soldiers, and destroy enemy supplies, bridges, and rail lines. Engineers who wanted to bring down structures quickly used dynamite to implode buildings.

But dynamite is also a tool for construction. Engineers use dynamite to cut openings through the mountains or hills to ease the building of highways, saving hundreds of hours of manual labor. We went to South Dakota this summer and learned that 90% of Mt. Rushmore was carved by dynamite. And dynamite has obviously been used in the mining industry to open up areas for exploration and use.

But what does that have to do with you? Well, the scriptures tell us God wants to express His power in us. The Greek word for power is *dunamis*, from which we get the word dynamite!

Peter says "His divine power has given to us all things that pertain to life and godliness..." (2nd Peter 1:3) So the power of God is sufficient for this moment, this day, this week, and this year, no matter what comes.

And God told Paul "My grace is sufficient for you, for My strength (power) is made perfect in weakness." (2nd Corinthians 12:9) Therefore, we cannot make the excuse that God cannot show His power in and through us because of our inabilities. All that matters is His ability, and with God all things are possible.

Finally, Jesus told the disciples, after reminding them that all authority and power (dunamis) had been given to Him in heaven and on earth (Matthew 28:18), that they would receive that power when the Holy Spirit came upon them so they could be His witnesses in Jerusalem, Judea, Samaria, and to the end of the earth. (Acts 1:8)

We sometimes don't think an explosion is a good thing, but the Lord wants you to explode where you are. If you know the Lord, and rely upon His Holy Spirit, you can be a positive agent of change wherever the Lord has placed you. You can help remove obstacles to building the highway of holiness, or you can help to open up new fields of understanding so you and others can mine God's word for gold nuggets of truth. You will be His witness to friends and family that God is not dead, and that faith is the victory that overcomes the world.

Do not let anything stop you from being used by God to change the spiritual landscape of your surroundings. He will even use the explosive power of the Holy Spirit within you to rout the enemy in spiritual warfare. You've been filled with dynamite. Explode for God's glory.

"Now to Him who is able to do exceedingly abundantly above all that we ask or think, *according to the power that works in us*..." (Ephesians 3:20—emphasis mine)

How To Enter Into Battle

War is an awful bloody thing. Paul Fussell discusses the stages of thinking in the men who enter battle in his book "Wartime". When considering the possibility of severe wounds or death, the average soldier's first rationalization is "It *can't* happen to me. I am too clever/agile/well-trained/good looking/beloved, etc." The second rationalization is : "It *can* happen to me, and I'd better be more careful. I can avoid danger by watching more prudently the way I take cover/dig in/expose my position by firing my weapon/keep extra alert at all times, etc." Finally, the realization is "It *is* going to happen to me, and only my not being there is going to prevent it."[59]

Well, only a relatively few Americans know experientially what it is like to face actual battle with real bullets, bombs, and imminent physical destruction. But if you are a believer, you know from much experience that Charles Spurgeon had it right when he said "conflict is the principle feature of the Christian life this side of heaven."[60] So which attitude mentioned above should the Christian take into the spiritual battles of life? Should we be cavalier and say "Satan can't touch me. I'm too clever/spiritually agile/beloved…?" Seems to me that's a good way for Satan to hand you your head on a plate. Our adversary may not be noble or respectable, but he certainly is crafty and knowledgeable, and he is utterly ruthless. Pride certainly goes before a fall. So then should we go into spiritual battle with the attitude that great wounding can happen to us, so we'd better avoid danger and basically try to hide from it? Sadly, if we approach spiritual battle that way, we are of little use to the kingdom of God and still can be run over by our enemy. We are to wield the shield of faith to quench the fiery darts and we are to wield the sword of the Spirit, and this is a picture of offensive warfare, not defensive digging in. Finally, is it best to realize "I am going to be wounded eventually, so the best thing to do is just not be there, just somehow find a way to be absent during the fight?" Many Christians seem to opt for this strategy, but what kind of life is it that runs from every battle and allows the enemy to ravage all those we love? Surely sooner or later, we must stand and fight.

So I am of the opinion that none of the options above are the best ones when we go into battle. All through the Bible God tells us to have courage, that He has not given us a spirit of fear, that the righteous are bold as a lion, and that having done all we are to stand against the wiles of our ancient foe. Being casual or dismissive in battle is foolish, but so is entering the battle thinking we can just hide in a foxhole and wait things out. And it is clear that if we are God's children we cannot shirk the battle altogether. Our own spiritual welfare and the welfare of those we care about most hinges on our ability to engage in warfare effectively. So we must enter the battle bravely, but wisely, trusting God to be our shield and defender. The battle belongs to the Lord, and He, the Lord of Hosts, will lead us to victory.

It Matters When You're There

This August for the first time in sixty years I can spend time working in my yard instead of being swallowed up in school-related activities.

And the yard looks better than it ever has before. It helps that God has sent the rain the last few weeks. No amount of watering can replace what rain does for the grass. Unfortunately, as you know, Bermuda grass isn't the only thing fond of rain. Johnson grass, grass-burs, goat-heads, and careless weeds are champion opportunists, and when rain comes down they grow up, *fast*.

So normally at this time of year I can't do much about it, because I'm at school, and when I get off school I still have papers to grade, lessons to prepare, and the like. But not this year. I can spend some time each day hoeing, spraying, and pulling the weeds, mowing the lawn, and taking care of things in better fashion. The yard doesn't look perfect; I've still got a long way to go with it; but it's in better shape than ever before, because I'm here to tend it.

How often do we get so busy with important things that we can't seem to find time to tend the gardens of our heart? In the parable of the Sower, Jesus said seed can sprout and grow on good soil, but some of that good soil gets covered over with "thorns" or weeds and although the person hears the word and tries to bear fruit, the "cares of this world" choke it out, and no fruit is borne. For our hearts to be the best kind of soil it must be continually tilled, softened, and weeded so that the yield can be thirty, sixty, or one hundred what was sown.

Be careful about letting important things crowd out essential things. It is easy to see what happens to a yard or garden—or a heart—that is neglected. The weeds take over, *quickly*. They are just looking for the chance to propagate. Make sure you are alert to their encroaching and take steps to remove them. Don't be an absentee gardener. The whole world notices the mess created when you're not there.

Not So Simple

Bryan Ganey had trouble getting to work one day. As he began to walk into the Verizon Call Center in Charleston, South Carolina for his normal shift, he began to gasp, collapsed in the bushes outside the building, and quickly called his mother Martha on his cell phone to get some help.

Bryan needed help. He weighed 577 pounds, and his life had been out of control for many years. His normal diet included skipping breakfast, eating fast food for lunch and dinner, and picking up some pizza on his way home...oh, and he also consumed more than a gallon of soft drink a day. By the age of 37 his body mass index was 87. Doctors consider 30 to be obese. He was very aware he had a problem, and doctors had already informed him that if he had a heart attack, which was likely, he was too large for an operation. That fateful day he was convinced the heart attack had finally come, and that he would soon be dead.

It was the best thing that could have happened to him. It was not a heart attack, but a pulmonary embolism, which is equally serious, but after six days in the hospital on blood thinners, the embolism cleared, and so did Bryan's head. Bryan turned from being a victim to being angry with himself for allowing his condition to deteriorate to this degree. *"My condition was unacceptable,"* he said. Doctors talked to him about weight-loss surgery, but he refused. He resolved to stay away from hospitals if at all possible. But how to shed all this weight?

He literally began with small steps, pushing a shopping cart around the grocery store like a toddler learning to walk. He started to walk out to the mailbox at the end of the driveway. Instead of riding everywhere, he took short walks to the park and around the neighborhood. Eventually he was conquering several miles at a time. He quit eating fast foods and skipping meals and drinking sodas, he started making his own meals of healthy meats, vegetables, and fruits. He now monitors closely his caloric intake and says "If you use more energy than you take in, you will lose weight." It's hard to be disciplined, because "food is everywhere, and I can't have just a little bit of bad foods. But the benefits I have gained...the prize is worth the struggle."

Bryan's goal is to get down to 200 pounds, and he has entered and finished 10K races. His mother prays every day that God will give him another day. She knows the obstacles addicts face in conquering their habits.[61]

It all seems so simple. Moderate exercise, good diet, avoid excesses—it's a good recipe for all of us to improve our health. But we know that this story inspires us precisely because the simple things in life are not always the easy things in life to do. It's one thing to have knowledge. It's another to apply wisdom. Bryan's near-death wakeup call gave him the motivation he needed to act wisely. Let's hope we don't need one to wake us up too.

Passing in Review

It was 1942, and the Japanese army battalion had set a new military record by marching in full gear 100 miles in 72 hours. American Colonel Robert Sink read about it and thought, "My men can do better than that." He chose the 2nd battalion under Major Robert Strayer to prove it. The 1st and 3rd battalions rode the 118 miles from Camp Toccoa, Georgia, to Ft. Benning in Atlanta. The 2nd battalion marched.

Dressed in full gear, carrying rifles, mortars, and machine guns; marching over back roads slippery with mud, pelted by cold rain and snow, through daylight and dark; it was an incredible feat daunting enough for any iron man. They covered 40 miles the first 16 hours, and collapsed in the field to sleep. They had to take shoelaces off boots the next morning just to get them back on over their swollen feet. The second day they covered another 40 miles, and some soldiers felt more dead than alive at day's end. But the third day was the worst. They still had 38 miles to go, the last 20 of them on a paved highway.

Pavement sounds like a godsend to men who had slipped in mud more than 90 miles, but the hard surface caused excruciating pain in the men's feet. By now they all hobbled. They camped on the outskirts of Atlanta in preparation for their triumphal entry the next morning, and when they were called to eat supper, Private Don Malarkey found he couldn't stand up; so he crawled on his hands and knees to chow, because he certainly wasn't going to miss getting his vittles. His platoon leader, Lieutenant Dick Winters, told him that he could ride in the ambulance the next morning to the final destination in downtown Atlanta.

But Malarkey decided the next morning that he could make it, and so did nearly everyone else. They wanted to march in beside their buddies, and they were so close to their objective, so the crippled men had extra motivation to see the task through to the end. But they still were terribly footsore, a pitiful sight as they set out the next morning. Word spread via radio and in the papers about the historic march, so crowds lined the route, cheering them on. Major Strayer also arranged for a band to play when they got to within a mile of their destination. When Malarkey—who was suffering terrible pain—heard the band, he said a remarkable thing happened. *"I straightened up, the pain disappeared, and I finished the march as if we were passing in review at Toccoa."*[62]

Life is a long, forced march. It leaves us footsore and we often wonder if we will have the strength to make it to the end. We don't want to be left behind; we want to pull our weight and fulfill our responsibilities; we know those next to us on the journey are also suffering greatly; we are often crippled by our experiences. But when we pass in review, hear the cheers of those who have gone before, catch the notes of the heavenly choir welcoming us home, we then will realize, as the scripture promises, that our afflictions will seem light compared to the glory that will be revealed. We will "pass in review," the Lord will say, "Well done!", and the pain will disappear...forever.

Perspective

Do you remember what it was like to be seventeen? Young and athletic and free from adult worries and cares? It was an idyllic time for me; carefree really. My biggest concerns were trying to understand girls and what to do with my spare time.

That was Caleb Freeman's experience too at seventeen. He was in high school, the best cross country runner on his 4A team, a starter in basketball, a young man with his entire bright future ahead of him. He was growing up in a stable Christian home where he felt secure and loved.

Until December of that year, when he and his brother Clayton were driving to an OU basketball game, and his vehicle hydroplaned, spinning him into the path of an 18-wheeler. Clayton emerged with a concussion, but for Caleb it was life-threateningly serious. The EMT crew working the scene called in the fatality team, and they shared that grim news with the parents. His father Jeremy was a pastor, so the family immediately went to prayer, but it was almost more than his mother could take. The Freemans had lost a 7-year-old son a few years previous, and she thought, "Lord, if you're going to take Caleb, take me too. I can't handle this twice."

To everyone's amazement, Caleb survived, but the outlook was bleak. With a severely damaged brain the doctors said he might never wake up, and if he did he wouldn't recognize anyone in the family or be able to eat or drink or talk on his own ever again. Caleb was in a coma for eight long weeks, with the family praying fervently. They knew the odds were stacked against them, but God was faithful. *"But God..."* became their motto.

The progress has been excruciating slow, but Caleb awoke from his long sleep, was able to recognize his family, has learned to eat, drink, walk, and talk again, and is making progress. But the most amazing thing about Caleb is his attitude. He and his father shared their story at our kids' camp recently, and the testimony is so powerful there was hardly a dry eye in the house. Caleb is witty, and although you have to struggle to understand him, he is laser-intense on sharing the love of Christ with others. When his father asked the nearly 200 campers if Caleb had told them that week that Jesus loved them, virtually every hand in the audience shot up. Jeremy asked Caleb if he could go back and change anything—if he could turn back the clock and become a perfectly healthy 17-year-old athlete again—would he do it? Caleb's answer was shocking. "No way," he said. "My story is being used by the

Lord to lead many people to Christ. I used to live mostly for my own glory. Now I live only to give glory to Jesus." [63]

Wow! What a reminder to us of Jesus' words: "He who finds his life will lose it, and he who loses his life for My sake will find it." Caleb certainly believes that. He seemingly had everything before, but wasn't focused on the Lord. Now that he is focused completely on the Lord, he realizes that all the other stuff is just stuff, and that his life now is much more exciting and fulfilling than before, despite his setbacks and challenges. What a great perspective Caleb has about life, and it gave all of us who heard him a fresh perspective as well.

Short-term-itis

A disease can be thought of as a condition that gets in the way of health. Given this definition a lot of people have a disease that gets in the way of their mental, emotional, spiritual, and financial health. It is called "short-term-itis." This disease is the problem of not having definite, challenging (but attainable and worthwhile) goals. It turns out too few people engage in long-range planning.

They want to improve their vocabulary and ability to think critically. They want to be financially secure, or get a better job, or improve their health by losing weight; or they want to engage in regular exercise. They want to understand the Bible better. But to achieve those aims specific goals are necessary. How much time a day will you allot to reading so your vocabulary and thinking skills can improve? How much money will you invest, and what will you invest in, to reach your goal of financial security? What training do you need to qualify for that better job? What would the appropriate resume look like so you could apply for it? How many miles a day do you want to walk to improve your health and lose that weight? How many minutes a day will you spend studying your Sunday school lesson so you can understand the Bible better?

There is more success when you have a definite goal, then *backtrack* to find out what steps you apply to reach that goal. One of my sons is a medical doctor. How do you become a doctor? Well, you need to be an intern first; but to be an intern you have to go through medical school. But wait, they don't just let anyone into medical school, so you have to study and pass a difficult test to be accepted to medical school. To practice studying, you could be getting a college degree in a tough field, like biochemistry, to prepare you for this more difficult schooling. It would also be helpful if you made good grades in your subjects to prove you are studying; tough courses in biology, chemistry, and other sciences.

All this implies of course that you gain entrance to the college in the first place, which requires you to do well on college entrance exams. This helps you win scholarships so you can pay for your education. Which brings you all the way back to high school, and determines what courses you will take there and how diligently you will apply yourself to be successful there, because it takes a lot of maturity and time to prepare for those huge tests coming up during college, medical school, and your internship. The steps a person takes today are determined by their long-term goals.

So we see that the behavior of a 16-year-old can be explained by goals (or the lack of them). Does he spend all his time playing video games or hanging out with friends, or does he spend a considerable amount of time in study? It depends on whether he has long-range thinking or is succumbing to short-term-itis. And this principle applies not just to the teenager, but to the adult as well. Even for those who have achieved many of their long-term goals, there is opportunity every day to establish other worthy goals. We are never done with setting and reaching goals until they bury us. What rewarding and valuable goals are you working toward this year?

Stay Focused

If you've ever looked carefully at animals, you've noticed that prey animals like deer, mice, rabbits, and squirrels all have eyes that are very widespread across the face. This allows them to have, in a sense, "wrap-around" vision. They aren't very good at bringing things into focus, but they are extremely good at picking up motion from not only the front of their bodies but also the sides. This ability keeps them alive many times as they sense a predator moving in.

For the predators what do you see? Eyes that face forward. They need to be able to focus on their prey, judge distance, and be able to help them close in on lunch. It is an awe-inspiring thing to watch in slow motion as a predator stalks and then attacks the next meal. The eyes are incredibly focused.

Talk-show host Michael Medved was fond of saying to a listener, "Let's focus like a laser beam." [64] It's the way to really understand something, and it's the way to reach a goal. The problem with many people in setting and reaching (or not reaching) goals is they try to get to the goal like a mouse would...instead of focusing they dilute their energies by looking at the things around them, the things that distract. They jump every time there is movement.

Don't be a mouse. Instead be like the owl, the tiger, or the lion. Once they lock in on their target, they stay focused until the target is reached. The fastest way to reach goals is to let nothing break your concentration. Stay focused.

SPLAT!

A seeker was looking for success, and he wanted to experience it God's way. He wanted to honor God with his life and choose those things that glorified the Lord. He walked and walked down a road until he came to a fork with two choices, and there he met a wise man. "Which way should I go to honor the Lord and find my destiny?" The wise man didn't say a word, but pointed to the left fork.

"Thanks!" The man eagerly went down the left fork, singing a merry tune. A few moments later the sound of SPLAT reaches your ears. Staggering back up the road to the wise man and the fork, the bloodied seeker stops and asks the wise man again, "Which way did you say to go to find what I want?" Again, the silent wise man pointed to the left fork of the path.

With considerable more caution the injured seeker again went down the left road, and again after a bit you hear the sound of SPLAT! Barely making it back to the wise man, wondering whether the wise man has misled him, the seeker, beaten and sore, returns to the fork in the road.

"Twice I've asked you to help me find the road to God's will for me; twice you've pointed left and I've followed your directions, and twice I've been SPLATTED. How will I ever find my destiny this way!"

The wise man finally spoke: *"Your destiny is indeed down this path. You will find it just beyond SPLAT."*

The moral of the story is clear. If you think that you will find godly success without being SPLATTED—in marriage, in your education, in your career, in your parenting, in your spiritual life—then you are no wise man at all. Wise men keep going *after* the splat!

If ever millions of people on planet earth have been splatted, it's been the last couple of years. But until God takes us home we cannot give up. Quitting is always an option; but it's a very poor option. Keep on moving after splat, and see what the Lord has in store for you. You may have new horizons, a new dawning of some grand things. You also might get more of splat! And if you are a person who has experienced a lot of living, you understand it will surely be a bit of both dawnings and splattings! Just keep going no matter what. God gives grace to endure the splats of life.

The Myth of the Great Athlete

Athletics came hard to him in high school. His coach advised him to play on his musical talent and join the band. He didn't have the natural coordination and skills of most guys his age. When he went out for basketball in the 9th grade the coach asked him, "Why are you doing this to yourself?" He responded, "Perseverance is part of my personality." The coach wasn't impressed. "We're in the process of developing athletes for the high school, and *you're not one of them*."

The story has an interesting twist from that point on. Not only did the young athlete improve dramatically during his high school days, he ended up playing professional football. And not only did he play pro ball, he became a star, part of the 1960's Los Angeles Rams' "Fearsome Foursome." He ended up playing his entire 15-year career with the Rams, and when it was over, Merlin Olsen was selected as a member of the Pro Football Hall-of-Fame.[65] Pretty good for a guy who was dismissed as no good by coaches when he was a young high school player.

His contention was that the "great athlete" is a myth. In the end it is hard work and perseverance that pays off, a willingness to keep on improving your craft to the best of your ability. Another example is the player who was benched his freshman and sophomore years in college, who watched as others led the team to glory. His college stats for those first two years weren't exactly impressive: -14 yards rushing, 129 yards passing, no touchdowns, and one interception. His junior year was better, but he shared playing time with another player his senior year. Still not awe-inspiring. And it got worse. His performance in the NFL Scouting Combine was historically dismal. Hoping to go in the first or second round of the NFL draft, his stock fell, and he was drafted in the 6th round. Most 6th round guys, if they even make a team, don't last long in the NFL. They just aren't good enough.

The quarterback had little hope for playing time his rookie season, designated fourth-string behind another rookie, an experienced backup, and the starter, who had played in three Pro Bowls. That year he played in one game, completed one pass, and watched as the other rookie quarterback played in eight games. Another 6th round bust, right? Not hardly. His second pro season, two of his competitors were gone and he entered the season as the backup. In the second game of that season the Pro Bowl quarterback was seriously injured, and Tom Brady was now the starter.

Now, at 43, he is the most successful pro quarterback of all time, hands down. He has 34 playoff wins, and Joe Montana, in second place, has 16. He has been to ten Super Bowls, winning seven of them, both records for a quarterback. Tom's secret to success? There are lots of them probably, but one is his work ethic. One coach said he is the hardest player ever to coach because he wants to know everything, and you'd better be ready to help him, because he's always ready to learn.

Natural? Gifted? Maybe. But most great athletes, and those who accomplish a lot in other fields, are those who work the hardest to become great.

The PR

Back in junior high and high school days our coaches wanted us to run track. In those days I never understood track. If there had been a 20-yard dash competition I might have been in the running, but blessed with short legs, I couldn't contend in the longer races built for peers with longer strides. I thought the purpose of track was to beat the other guys in the 100-yard or 200-yard dash, and I knew I couldn't beat them, so why bother? Coaches put me in the 880-yard run, but again it wasn't a pretty sight. My only claim to fame was that I never finished last in a race; but boy I was nowhere near the front either. When coaches don't know where to race you they put you in the hurdles, and for one very brief moment of glory I was in the lead halfway through a heat, dreaming of being Jim Thorpe, when I tripped over the next to last hurdle, bloodied my knees on the cinder track, and all dreams of ribbons aside, I retired to the bus to nurse my wounds and vow to never run track again.

I missed the whole point. There is a reason coaches of other sports want students to run track. I thought the object was to beat the other guy; but the object of track was to teach me to beat *me*. That's where the PR comes in. PR stands for ***personal record***. It's probably not a record that someday graces the record board at school; it's a record for you, a record that you learned to better yourself regardless of what others have accomplished. When people push themselves, better themselves, improve on their own performance, it's a win, isn't it? In a basketball book called *Stuff* by Dick DeVenzio he asked the question "Who can you beat?" with the profound answer, *"You, yesterday."*[66] It's a very simple idea, but one that has application in any field and at any age.

You may not be Einstein, but you can know more than you knew yesterday if you'll take the time to learn more today. You may not be able to play that piano like Chopin, but you can practice to play it better than you did last week. You may not have the greatest relationship with a family member today, but you can do something today to have a better relationship tomorrow. Perhaps today you can't walk a mile without losing your breath, but can you walk a half-mile? It may be that the only person who is impressed with your accomplishment is you, but there's nothing wrong with that.

And it's also amazing how many people are cheering you on in your pursuit of your PR. My brother has competed in triathlon competitions, where a person runs, bikes, and swims. He said he was taken aback by the number of other competitors who encouraged everyone to give it their best, to "go for the gold", even though for them the gold was just finishing the race in 32nd place and getting to go eat at Texas Roadhouse. The only question for them was, "Did I improve; am I still chasing a new PR?"

Louise Adams of Colorado had worked to continually improve her PR, finding such success that she qualified for the 2007 World Masters Championships. Fulfilling a lifelong dream, she won a gold medal, finishing first in the 5000 meter run in those games.[67] Okay, full disclosure, she happened to be the only competitor in the race, she didn't quite finish, and had to be given medical attention. But she was 86-years-old at the time, pushing herself to her limits with only herself to beat. Can we hear a loud cheer for a lady who hasn't given in to the temptation to quit setting and reaching new goals? Who can you beat? **You, yesterday.**

The Theory of Relativity

I've always loved adventure stories. When I was growing up I enjoyed classics like *Treasure Island, The Adventures of Tom Sawyer, Huck Finn, 20,000 Leagues Under the Sea, Mysterious Island,* and the like. One of my early favorites was Daniel Defoe's *Robinson Crusoe.* Think of it. To be marooned on a desert island and have to fight for survival against hunger, the elements, and loneliness; how dreadful that would be. I couldn't help but put myself in that situation and wonder how I would handle it. I decided to reread the book not long ago, and was reminded of a principle that is true in the life of every person.

Crusoe spent many months fashioning a dugout canoe so he could sail around his island and view it from the ocean. He got everything prepared for his short voyage, and was off to circumvent the island, when all of a sudden he encountered a strong current which swept him out to sea. His sail and homemade paddle were useless in trying to gain control of the craft, and the island receded from view. Frantically he prayed to God for deliverance, and miles from shore the current abated a bit and he was able to make his way back to the sandy beach. In gratitude he threw himself down and thanked God profusely, and he realized this significant truth: what had been in his mind a horrible fate, being alone on an island, was so much better than being lost at sea to die of thirst and starvation, that the one place he had desired to leave with all his heart became the place he desired to return to with all his heart.[68] Compared to death in the canoe, life on the island was a paradise.

We all experience the same thing. Our children are too loud and rambunctious, but if one of them lay lethargically in intensive care fighting a losing battle with leukemia, we would give the world to see them up making noise and happily playing. Our spouse irritates us and perhaps nags us a bit too much; but the lonely widow or widower would give anything to have a companion with whom to share life. Our job isn't the greatest in the world and we can think of all the hard things about it; but if we were unemployed, struggling to survive on government largesse, bereft of the tasks that give order and meaning to our lives, how hard would it be? Life and happiness are always *relative*, aren't they? We complain about not having enough money for this or that, when compared to billions of people all across the globe we are unbelievably wealthy. We gripe because COVID-19 caused us to miss out on our vacation, while a poor subsistence farmer in Africa doesn't even know what a vacation is because he's never had one. We end up in the hospital for surgery and are feeling sorry for ourselves until we room with another who is dying in pain. We will be released in a few days. His only release is in death.

Do we have situations that aren't perfect, that frustrate us? Are we tired of the hassles of life, the hardships, the obstacles that block our progress? Of course. But think how very many ways it could be worse. We must be grateful for what we have, and content with the situations that are unchangeable. It's all relative, and relatively speaking, we have it pretty good.

Chapter Six—
The People Who Run Things

The only thing more amazing than the depth of the corruption of our politicians is the foolishness of the electorate. From the birth of our nation Americans have complained about the leadership of their leaders, and then they refuse to vote on Election Day or they do vote and elect a yet more corrupt person to a post than the person before. It's hard for an old codger like me to think about how far down the road to Socialism we've traveled, but the real problem with government is not the name of the system it uses. As one wag put it, *"under capitalism, man exploits man. Under communism it's just the opposite."*[69] Ultimately all governments will have corruption because the Bible says people are corrupt without God. Both Old and New Testaments tell us that no one is good, no, not one (Psalm 14, Psalm 53, and Romans 3). Ranting and raving against our leaders doesn't seem to accomplish much, but there is a smidgen of therapy in it, so here goes...

Anybody Else Confused?

This may not be the most horrific of times. We complain a lot about our present situation, but compared to Black Plagues, world wars, and the horrors of ancient civilizations that destroyed each other completely we have it pretty good. Nevertheless, at best this is a confusing time. We were told at the beginning of the COVID pandemic that masks don't help, then told later that they do help, then told we MUST wear them to keep everyone alive, then told that we need to wear two or three masks at a time to insure everyone's safety, even after vaccination. And some told us all along they didn't help.[70] We are told that this is the worst epidemic of all time, even though there is more than a 99% survival rate.[71]

We were told that we must be in lockdown and stay at home; then found out that the safest places to be were outside and not cooped up in homes.[72] We were told that COVID-19 was so serious that you would certainly know it if you got it; that it was a death sentence; until we found out you could have it and carry it and spread it but not have the remotest idea you had it.[73] We've been told that vaccines were perfectly safe, until recently when they pulled the Johnson and Johnson vaccine for causing serious problems in people who already had the virus circulating in their systems. [74] We were told to assiduously wash everything we touched, until it came out that the virus really didn't linger on surfaces much.[75] We were told to flatten the curve, then all would return to normal, but after flattening we remained in trouble.[76] We were told to stay away from restaurants, then were told to wear masks as we enter the restaurants but take the masks off while we eat (makes sense).[77] We were told millions in Florida and Texas would die because their governors were so irresponsible for removing many of the mandates that impinged on freedoms and destroyed businesses—that didn't happened either—in fact, the states with the most coronavirus problems remain the blue states where the most egregious mandates have remained in place.[78]

Confused yet? It sort of feels like we've been put in a big washing machine on the spin cycle and the world has spun out of control. Politicians are incredibly inept, extremely diabolical, or both at the same time, depending on your view. It is a certainty that they realized a great opportunity for a power grab, and they don't want to let go. They love telling others what to do and having them obey like little robots. Many have specialized in "Rules for thee, but not for me."

Life has been so strange it's comforting to know that when God tells you something in His Word, he doesn't change the story later on. Psalm 119:89 says His Word is forever settled in heaven. It is a sure guide to life; just as sure today as it has ever been. I don't know about you, but I'm glad for some straight talk that doesn't change with every political wind.

Political Animals

Men and women without God are driven to rule over one another. Jesus told His disciples that they must learn to serve others in order to be great instead of trying to lord it over each other in a mad scramble for power and riches (Matthew 20:26). There is no question in my mind that today in America we are governed by the worst set of rascals in our long history. Aesop, the famous moralist, once quipped that we hang petty thieves and appoint the great ones to public office.[79] When you see how much money members of Congress make by being in their positions you see why Aesop was so pessimistic. Some have said instead of giving politicians the key to the city, maybe we should change the lock![80]

In our country, as Oscar Ameringer once said, "Politics is the gentle art of getting votes from the poor and campaign funds from the rich, by promising to protect them from each other."[81] Boy, have some of our politicians perfected this art! When you have a populace that gets hooked on receiving goodies from government, you have a readymade mess that gets worse every year. Our political system has become very proficient at taking things from those who earned them so they can give those things to those that haven't earned them—after they skim off their own take, of course. Texas Guinan said "A politician is a fellow who will lay down your life for his country."[82] (emphasis mine) We have learned a lot about *"Rules for thee, but not for me"* during the COVID lockdowns.

As Plato once opined, "those who are too smart to engage in politics are punished by being governed by those who are dumber."[83] Why in the world do we allow it? Beats me, but if the government told us it would be best for us to prevent COVID spread, I believe half the country would load up their children on a train and send them away...somewhere. How foolish and naïve can we get? Apparently pretty foolish and naïve. Even the Russians understand politicians better than we do.

Nikita Khruschchev once said "Politicians are the same all over. They promise to build a bridge even where there is no river."[84] And people fall for the ruse over and over. Maybe it's true that a sucker is born every minute. I'm afraid that well over half the world's suckers live in our country. John Quinton adds this, that "Politicians are people who, when they see light at the end of the tunnel, go out and buy some more tunnel."[85] Of course they do. It's not their money they spend. And they seemingly never get around to asking us whether we want that extended tunnel or not.

Clarence Darrow once said "When I was a boy I was told that anybody could become President. I'm beginning to believe it."[86] Given the current conditions in our country this is one of those jokes that is too funny because it's too true.

Self-Interest?

Nobody wants to be thought of as selfish or self-centered. We are taught that this is the essence of sinfulness. But there is a sense in which knowing and taking care of self becomes a force for positivity in society. How so? Well, selfishness *is* a toxic thing in any society. When everyone only looks out for #1, conflict is guaranteed and conflict resolution becomes virtually impossible. But *enlightened* self-interest is another thing altogether.

Here's an example. As an educator I have tried to give the interests of others a high priority. I have cared deeply about students and their families for decades, and done what I could to support and guide them toward a better life. Forced to choose, however, between students in my class and my own children, my own children rank higher in priority and must therefore be cared for first, even if others have unmet needs. On the surface this seems a selfish choice; maybe the most altruistic thing to do would be to care for a student regardless of their relationship to me. But on reflection nearly all people, given a real choice between caring for family or caring for others not in the family, would choose family first. In a real sense we believe it is our duty to do so, and this is biblically sound. I Timothy 5:8 says "Anyone who does not provide for their relatives, and especially for their own household, has denied the faith and is worse than an unbeliever." According to Adam Smith this is a type of *neutral* self-interest. It does not seek to harm another, but simply to order priorities of the care each individual gives to others in a way that conscience dictates.[87]

So responsibility for taking care of the welfare of others begins at home. And this is a wonderful thing for society as well. If I not only take care of the physical needs of my own children, but also train them to behave properly in society and bring benefit to the society, then society isn't burdened with trying to care for them or deal with their misdeeds. If my children are properly provided for and trained to provide for themselves, they won't ever be in the food line or needing public welfare to meet their needs. Trained to respect authority, they won't be part of the mob looting or rioting in the streets. Think of the money, time, and treasure the society *saves* by not having to deal with my children using a government program!

In a perfect world (the kind of world God originally created but man destroyed) there would be a nuclear family that met the needs of its members and trained its members to be contributing ("adding", as opposed to destructive or "subtracting") members of society. We wouldn't need lots of welfare programs or Big Brother/Big Sister programs at that point, would we? When parents engage in enlightened self-interest, taking care of the needs of the immediate family, it ends up becoming a very positive thing for society as a whole.

It is at that point, the point where family needs are met, that a person can turn their attention to *others,* others who *don't* have that family structure or support. Adam Smith argues that benevolence is desirable "only after individuals have attended to their own self-interest. *Only after they have taken care to ensure that they and those who depend on them are adequately clothed, housed, and educated can they turn their eyes to benevolently helping others outside their intimate circle.*"[88] Since we obviously live in a fallen rather than perfect world, there will always be young people who need leadership, support, and resources to help them. Their family unit is too dysfunctional to provide these things. But don't assume that men and women who put family first are selfish for doing so. Their enlightened self-interest becomes the greatest gift they can give the larger culture, a child who is whole and unbroken, a child that has no need for government programs at all.

Self-Interest and Socialism

Adam Smith, a 17th-century Scottish philosopher and economist, wrote *The Wealth of Nations*, one of the most influential books ever penned. He argued when two entities are involved in a free exchange of goods or services, both entities can benefit. Smith's ideas greatly impressed the Founding Fathers and led to the greatest economic system in world history. Smith taught that individual self-interest caused each party in a business deal to seek to maximize their own benefit, and while this sounds selfish (as Smith's critics say), it actually encourages a virtue that protects both individuals in the deal.[89]

Smith believed the conscience (the "impartial spectator") would prevent most people from allowing their own self-interest to harm others. The conscience imposes external limits on self-interest motivated by guilt, and by the "disapprobation" of society, because most people want to be seen as benevolent, not self-centered. The fear of societal rejection was enough to keep most people honest in their dealings with others.[90] Proverbs 22:1 says it this way, "A good name is to be chosen above all riches." Smith said that pursuing self-interest without justice wouldn't work because "justice is the main pillar that upholds the whole edifice...if it is removed, the fabric...of human society must in a moment crumble to atoms."[91] Selfishness ignores justice and seeks to gain for self no matter the harm done to others. Self-interest *embraces* justice and only seeks to achieve its own goals without harming others.

Smith made clear that self-interest is *not* vicious, self-centered behavior that destroys community, but rather the key to producing stable, just, and orderly societal interactions which allow people to pursue their own goals without impeding the pursuit of everyone else to achieve theirs. Let's illustrate. You go to the grocery store to buy milk. You have worked at your job so you have money to spend, and you can spend it how you wish. Today you wish to buy milk for your family because your kids are eating cereal for breakfast. You buy the milk, giving the cashier money. That money is a trade: your work for a gallon of milk. It is to your interest to purchase the milk; your family will enjoy it and benefit from it. But purchasing the milk helps pay the dairy farmer who milked the cow, the truck driver who picked up and delivered the milk, the owner of the grocery store, the stocker and cashier who work at that store, and it even helps the cow, because the dairy farmer can buy food for her. Your self-interest has indirectly met the self-interest of a plethora of others. You didn't particularly think of them when you went to the store, but your self-interest and their self-interest intersected, and everyone benefits. This is how capitalism works.

Socialism, on the other hand, sounds wonderful but never works. In this system everyone is supposed to work hard to benefit everyone else's interest. And you would think, especially in a culture rooted in Judeo-Christian values, that this system would work fine. The trouble is that nobody really wants to work to meet the interests of those far removed from them. The idea of helping "society" is too remote for us. We understand the idea that our child wants milk for their cereal. It's harder to appreciate helping a large mass of "others" we don't know, or somehow aiding the "government", whoever they are. People are naturally and highly motivated to meet their own needs and the needs of those immediately in their sphere of influence (especially their family). Socialism by its very nature de-motivates because interests don't often intersect, at least not in tangible, clear ways. Socialism, wherever it has been tried, ends up meeting the interests of an elite ruling class while enslaving a large ruled class. Socialist countries have no "middle" class, only rich and powerful "haves", and lots of poor "have-nots."

Adam Smith argued that it is because they neglect the important motivation of self-interest. The Pilgrims tried a socialist experiment in the early days of America.[92] Everyone worked a community garden to give to whoever had need. What happened? You could guess it. A few individuals realized that they could be lazy and receive welfare benefits without having to put out. The experiment ended in abject failure, and the Protestant work ethic emerged, where an enterprising worker could better himself and his family because his self-interest was rewarded by the fruits of his labor. The resulting country these hard workers created, the United States of America, built on this capitalistic ideal, became the wealthiest nation for the most people in the history of the world. Enlightened self-interest wins out over Socialism every time.

Three Judgments

There are two judgment seats described in Scripture. The most fearful of them is the Great White Throne judgment related in Revelation 20; the judgment of those who have never given their lives to Christ. Punishment here is meted out to those who have rejected God's way of salvation, where those not found in the Lamb's Book of Life are removed from God's presence. What a fearful fate! But there is another judgment seat that Paul tells us about in Romans 14 and 2nd Corinthians 5—the judgment seat of Christ. This is the place where *believers* are judged "according to what they have done in the body…"

Jesus mentions this judgment in Matthew 16:27 when He says "For the Son of Man will come in the glory of His Father with His angels, and then He will reward each according to His works." Ephesians 2:10 tells us God has prepared good works for us to do after we are saved, works "which God prepared beforehand that we should walk in them." Salvation is always by grace through faith, and all three of these (salvation, grace, and faith) are gifts of God that cannot be earned or merited.

But after experiencing salvation we are to use the gifts God gives us (the talents, time, spiritual gifts) to serve Him on this earth. This time on earth is critical for "laying up treasures in heaven, where neither moth nor rust corrupts, and thieves do not break in and steal." (Matthew 6:20) Before Paul mentions the Bema seat judgment of believers he previews how we should see the trials and hardships on earth, as "light" and "for a moment" *compared to* the rewards we will receive for eternity for pressing on in Christ despite our afflictions. (2nd Corinthians 4:17) The great news about this judgment seat is that, although we should prepare for it soberly as a time of accounting for our lives, and though there will undoubtedly be some tears of regret that we didn't serve the Lord more faithfully, it is a time of reward and not punishment. Our sins were punished by God when He laid them on Jesus at the cross. Christ died *once for all* (I Peter 3:18). For the believer, the punishment of sin is a *past* event, not a future one (thank God!) So serve the Lord with gladness and enter into the works He has for you today to honor His name. Your reward will be great in heaven.

There is a third judgment not directly mentioned in Scripture. It is the judgment of God on America, and part of that judgment occurs on Election Day. Supposedly, a woman asked Benjamin Franklin what kind of government the Constitutional Convention had given them, and his reply was "A Republic, if you can keep it." [93] The quote has been uttered by both Democrats and Republicans, but what does it mean? Well, a Republic is a form of government where people vote to elect representatives to enact laws that govern the country. A Republic is a system of government under *law*. Following these ideals has allowed the U.S. to have a peaceful transition of power, despite vigorous and angry disagreements over policy, for 250 years. Watching the news this year we have become aware that this tradition is in grave danger. A fairly large portion of the nation has decided that if it doesn't like something, it will tear it down or burn it down instead of trying to win elections or enact laws. Many of our large cities have become havens for anarchy, rioting, and looting. And government officials have allowed it to happen, ordering police to stand down and resisting help from federal officials who want to restore law and order. These things in themselves are a form of judgment from God. They are reminders that we often get exactly what we deserve in our country, since we have the power to elect the officials we want. Their power is simply an extension of our will.

Hopefully voters will oust the incompetent, the corrupt, and the elites who refuse to care for those they govern. I'm not convinced at all that will happen, however. When voters foolishly re-elect bungling leaders, they merit the chaos that follows. God help us all to pass this judgment day by exercising sound judgment when we vote. And God help us keep our Republic.

Chapter Seven—
Gotta Love Your Family

As a teacher and a preacher I often tell stories about my family. The stories emphasize lessons we can learn about life. Having eleven children makes for an enormous wealth of anecdotes, and believe me, I make good use of them as illustrations. Of course I often use anecdotes from my relationship with my wife Gwynne as well. Oftentimes the stories are humorous examples of important spiritual principles. God gave us a family for a lot of reasons, and if we will learn from them we will become more of what we were created to be. I am indebted to my wonderful wife and to my eleven wonderful children for teaching me so much about life. And at this writing I am indebted to my seventeen grandchildren for highlighting many of those lessons once again. In our family we try to learn important things from everyday events and circumstances. I've even learned quite a few lessons from my dog! He certainly is part of our family.

Big Shoes to Fill

Today I have many grandchildren, and I am so thankful. I get to learn many life lessons watching them grow up, like I once learned by watching my own children. Sometimes when a child is rather small and perhaps immature, we wonder what they will be when they grow up. Will they be part of this world's problems or its solutions? Hopefully the latter. Will they ever be able to fill our shoes?

My youngest son had some red boots that he loved to wear when he was little. They got really worn and torn, but he was still proud of them, and he was so cute wearing them. Now his feet are bigger than mine. It used to be that my shoes were much too large for him to wear—now he can't fit into them because they are too small. And he has become a leader of others. God has blessed him with younger teens who look up to him and strive to be like him. He is especially admired among the younger kids at our church. Every Wednesday night and Sunday morning, instead of asking what a great message I have ready to share with them, they invariably ask "Where's Josiah?"

So we sometimes wonder when our children are younger if they will ever grow up and be able to fill our shoes. Turns out that much of the time they become so admirable of character that others are trying hard to fill theirs.

It's Because of Her

I was visiting with an adult before our Sunday morning service recently when a bright, perky six-year-old tugged at my coat. "Mr. Howard, I have my Bible verse ready." I had challenged some children with the task of memorizing eight Bible verses, and told them I'd give them $10 if they completed all of them. This was her sixth verse. She dutifully recited it, and I expressed my delight in her diligence and knowledge. The little girl didn't hesitate at all, but pointed to her mother who was standing about ten feet behind us. "It's my mom," she admitted.

Profound, isn't it. And not surprising. The challenge of memorizing the verses had been given to ten students. Only one learned every verse and earned the money, and you don't have to guess who it was. Despite being the youngest person in the class the little girl finished all eight verses and shared the final one with the whole congregation. She did so because she is exceptionally capable and has a wonderful, engaging personality. But more than that, she finished the task, earned the money, and completed the goal because she had a mother who encouraged her, worked with her, and insisted on her using her God-given intellect to do something worthwhile.

Many of us, when we look back, can point to a mother or father (or both), and say, "I am what I am in large part because of her (or him, or them)." They say that life is hard, and certainly in many ways that is true, but finding success in life isn't really that hard. When mothers and fathers are engaged in training their children, when they take the time and put forth the effort to make goal-setting and accomplishment part of their normal parenting process, the results are usually satisfying. This same girl took part in a cattle show not long ago, and earned fifth place in her event. That is outstanding, even when you consider there were only five students in her event. Her mother told me she was there to learn and grow. Goal reached. What do you bet this girl wins a first-place banner someday? You know, in many ways she's already a champion, in large part because she has godly parents that are training her to set and reach worthy goals in life.

Paul commended Timothy for his sincere faith, but then added this reflection, that the faith found in Timothy was first found in his mother Eunice and grandmother Lois. (2nd Timothy 1:5) When others noticed the strong faith in this young man, he quite possibly pointed out, "It's because of them." He would have properly credited his vibrant faith to faithful mentors who had trained him up so that he would be "wise unto salvation." (2nd Timothy 3:15) That dynamic was beautifully illustrated by our young friend not long ago. I hope and pray all parents will diligently teach their sons and daughters the ways of God. If America is to be reclaimed, it will be because of them.

Diligently teach them

Come Home

Our dog Max has been missing for more than a week. Normally obedient to stay in the yard, and normally returning soon if he ever does get out, Max did neither of those things recently. There have been several stray dogs roaming the neighborhood, and we figured that maybe he was intrigued by their carefree lifestyle and wanted to join them, ala *Lady and the Tramp*. We fretted and prayed, asked neighbors and friends from church; no one had seen him. He's a very friendly hound, so we thought maybe he had found a new home. But since he loves to chase birds, another likely scenario was that he got into somebody's chickens and paid the ultimate price for his transgressions. Surely *something* had happened to keep him from home.

We certainly don't worship our animals around here, but Max had wormed his way into our hearts. Even Gwynne was thinking of him often and distressed to see him gone. It takes a special animal to gain her affection, let me tell you. We had entered some of the stages of grief common to those who lose something they hold dear, and we were thinking about maybe getting another dog for Laura, although it would have been hard to replace Max in our affections. What bothered us most was that Max had left us. He had seemed content and "happy" for a dog. His waywardness distressed us greatly.

Well, this morning I was taking a walk to exercise, and on my way back home a pickup stopped and I chatted with a good friend from church. I showed him my walking stick, which was to ward off aggressive dogs and such, and he told me he had an extra dog at his house that somebody had "dropped off" for him. I told him of our prodigal dog and asked, "What kind of dog (meaning what breed)?" His answer, typical of his fun-loving spirit, was "Black." He said he could bring the dog over later if I wanted, and I told him I'd talk to Gwynne about it. He drove off and I walked on.

Later in the morning I had finished mowing the yard and was raking up grass when Gwynne came running into the yard followed by...you guessed it! MAX!! Our friend's mystery dog that someone had delivered to him was none other than our very own stray, brought home at last. Excited and thankful, we hugged Max and welcomed him home, got him some water and food, played with him and told him never to leave us again.

You remember when Christ said that the angels in heaven rejoice over one lost one who returns to the fold? How it grieves the Lord when we wander off, when we try to be "free" only to find ourselves in danger of destruction; and how the Lord and all His angels rejoice when we come home. We didn't berate Max for his wanderlust. We were just glad he was back. God feels that way about all who come home to Him.

Dedicated

To be dedicated is to be committed. Words or phrases that might be synonymous are wholehearted; single-minded; enthusiastic; zealous.[94] Several of my adult daughters are dedicated to learning how to take care of their families in a more natural, healthy way. They are learning to make yogurt, can vegetables and meats, make granola, create their own oatmeal, make avocado oil, use essential oils, and improve their food menus for their families. And they are evangelical about it. When they talk on the phone they are excited, they share new insights and abilities they are learning, they brainstorm new ideas. They are enthusiastic, zealous, and single-minded about this business. They are *serious*.

One daughter and her husband recently dedicated their infant son to the Lord during a church service. The child is blissfully unaware of this momentous occasion because he is only eight months old, but the parents feel it is important to dedicate him to the Lord, for the Lord's purposes in his life. Will it ultimately matter in the life of the child? Will it affect the outcome of his life when he is a teenager or young adult, when he will be free to decide for himself whether he wants to follow God's will for his life?

It can if his parents are dedicated too. Since an infant is too young to make a commitment of this importance, the real dedication is the dedication of the parents to the task of raising the child in the nurture and admonition of the Lord (Ephesians 6:4), to training up the child in the way he should go (Proverbs 22:6), to follow the instructions of Deuteronomy 6, where the Lord gives the parents in general and the father specifically the charge to teach the children the ways of God when going somewhere or staying at home, when rising and when getting ready for bed; at all times.

Samuel was dedicated to the Lord, but more important, Hannah was dedicated to fulfilling her promise to the Lord. In essence, what she said in I Samuel 1:28 must be the thinking of every parent with every child. "...I have lent him to the Lord; as long as he lives he shall be lent to the Lord." That's it. Dedicating our child to God shows that we recognize our child is a gift from God, lent to us to train and point back to God. Dedicating a baby to God does not secure their salvation or their sanctification. But it is a way of dedicating yourself to be a godly example to that child for the entirety of their lives, and it is a commitment you make with God to give (lend) your child back to God to do with as God sees fit. For most children, the dedication ceremony is most effective when the parents are also dedicated to raising them in a godly manner.

God Has the Copyright

Copyright refers to the legal right of the owner of intellectual property. In simpler terms, copyright is the right to copy. This means that the original creators of products and anyone they give authorization to are the only ones with the exclusive right to reproduce the work. [95]

My wife Gwynne made a great point in a talk we did last night for a group of young students at a Fellowship of Christian Athletes gathering after the football game. We were talking about how important it was to choose wisely when picking a marriage partner; how after our decision to follow Christ with our lives there was no more important or far-ranging decision than what we think about marriage and who we choose to marry. She said, "God invented marriage; He's the creator of the institution (Genesis 2), therefore He has the copyright on it. Only He can define it and tell us what it means, and no one else has the right to reproduce it."

How true. We are surrounded by a society that believes it can change institutions that have been around for thousands of years (marriage, the church, schools, civil authority) and make them whatever the progressive left wants to make them. But this is not their option, especially when it comes to the institution undergirding all the others in a civilized and humane society: marriage. Marriage is not marriage if it is between two women or two men, or if it is between a man and several women, or if it is anything other than a union between one man and one woman who take vows to love one another until one of them dies. It was God Himself who said one man shall leave father and mother and cleave unto his one wife and become one (Genesis 2:24 and quoted by Christ in Matthew 19:5). It is *together* that one man and one woman best help us see the image of God. It is not good for a man to be alone (Genesis 2:18). One way marriage can help young men is to challenge them to grow up and act like men, instead of behaving like little boys. Grown men take responsibility. Grown men care for others and put their needs before their own. Grown men get up, go to work, provide for their families, and return home to their families to play with them, teach them, and train them in the way they should go. When a young woman gives in to the whining little child that lives inside a male; when she allows him to indulge himself with her body without a marriage commitment, when she caves in to his wimpy complaints and wrongly strokes his ego, she does him no favors. The greatest need of a man in a relationship with a woman is to have her respect because he knows he has earned her respect.

Healthy marriages are vital for a society. Promote them. And be sure and define them the way God does. He has authorized you to reproduce the work He began so long ago. After all, He has the only copyright on it.

Insert image 4 here-Caption: Bruce and Gwynne Howard

Let 'em Fly!

On this wonderful day of thanksgiving we are surely thankful for our families, for our children and grandchildren. My son-in-law Seth recently preached a great sermon on Psalm 127:4-5 about them. All of his points were great, but the last point especially hit me. Speaking about arrows in the hands of a warrior (Psalm 127), he said that not only are our children our greatest legacy, but they are ours so we can prepare them to be *released*. We have to let them go, shoot them out into the world. That's where they'll have the biggest impact, make the most difference.

God calls us to be stewards of many things in this life, including our children. In a real sense they are never "ours", they always did belong to God, just as Samuel illustrates. Hannah "gave" Samuel to God, but in reality all children belong to Him. God gives us the task of training them in His ways to prepare them for the ministry He has for them. Once that training is over, we release them to the world, where they can be useful to the Lord who fights our battles for us.

Seth mentioned that trained correctly, our children fight evil, but they also fight *for us* because they

1) Defend us and speak highly of us (notice in Psalm 127:5 that we are not ashamed as we speak to others in the gate; in part because we are supported by children who speak up for us).
2) Pray for us. How wonderful to have adult children who are prayer warriors for the battles we face.
3) Care for us when we need them. Obviously this may be when we are old and frail, but it also is true that when we need resources we have our children who we can call on for help (just as they can still call on us for help).
4) Weep for us when we are gone. How sad the one who dies alone and un-mourned. Many of our old friends may pass before we do, but many others cannot or will not be able to attend our memorial service. Our children, however, will all make sure they are there.

Our children are meant to be sent. And so "Happy is the man who has a quiver full of them." (Psalm 127:5) We don't realize the impact they will have on the larger world. And we don't understand how quickly they are loaned to us and then called to go and make families and futures of their own. All we know is that we can't hang on to them. We always marvel at how fast they grow up, and we often want to slow time down, but it is the way God has planned it. Just like an unused arrow does a warrior no good, so a child not prepared to send out into the world is a waste. Train them up, parents! Then let 'em fly!

Arrows in the quiver

Run Your Race

The other day I went to watch a grandson compete in his junior high track meet. I've confessed before that I was not a huge fan of track when I was younger, feeling rather inadequate in the sport. Unfortunately, some of my grandchildren are following in my less than illustrious footsteps and are not big track fans either. Nevertheless, it was fun to go and spend time supporting his efforts and cheering him on.

Like most grandparents I enjoy capturing family moments on film, so I took along my camera. The grandson did the pole vault and ran in the 400-meter relay and the hurdles, and I dutifully snapped pictures. I love close-ups rather than pictures where you wonder who is in the picture, and as I cropped the pictures on the computer something dawned on me. When you focus on just one snapshot of one competitor it's very hard to tell if they are in first place or last place, whether they got over the bar on the pole vault or not.

And it reminded me that winning the event, although a noble goal, is not the usual result for most competitors. I never won a blue ribbon at a track meet, and so far none of my grandkids have either. That didn't change my willingness to travel many miles just to see my grandson's efforts, and it didn't change my patting him on the back and telling him he did a good job. He finished in the middle of the pack on the hurdles, for example, but my son-in-law tells me it's the third time he's ever run them, and one of those was at practice. You don't really expect world records to fall when the back story reads like that.

Paul told us in I Corinthians 9:24 that we are to run our race to obtain the prize. But the prize isn't a first place medal; the prize is the commendation of those who are watching the race, the approval of the audience. We have a great cloud of witnesses watching us run our race, and the most important audience of all, our Lord, who watches every step. They are cheering us on, and regardless of how many break the tape ahead of us, we can all run in such a way that we will hear "well done!" By the way, the grandson did medal in the pole vault, placing third. But if he had come in last place, I still would have been proud that he was in the competition instead of standing idly by on the sidelines. The fact that he was there, doing his best, was good enough for the father and the grandfather. Don't think your running does not matter just because you don't finish ahead of others. In a real sense, the competition is you giving the effort to outdo yourself yesterday.

The Impedimenta of War

An impediment is an obstruction or hindrance that keeps you from doing something. "He would go far except for his speech impediment." "These heavy taxes are an impediment to economic growth." "The enemy artillery has us pinned down and is a major impediment to our line of advance."

Interestingly the origin of the word does indicate something that slows you down but does *not* indicate something that is a hindrance. Wait! How can something slow you down but not be an obstacle or hindrance? Well, Julius Caesar talked about the impedimenta of war, the baggage that slows down the progress of an army. He was speaking of the thousand and one things an army takes with it besides men, things like food and medical supplies and extra uniforms and pencils and paper and building supplies for barracks' construction and electric wire and phones and other communications devices and heavy coats for winter fighting and Bibles and paper clips and staplers and bullets and tanks and guns and... For a large army there are hundreds of thousands of tons of materiel that goes along as well.[96]

It's mind-boggling. It would be kind of nice I guess if fighting men could just show up and be free of all that stuff so they could move faster and take the battle to the enemy. Tens of thousands of hours are spent loading and unloading and taking care of all those things that "slow the army down." The problem of course is that in war one of the cardinal principles is that an army should never outrun its supply lines. No matter how much progress is being made against the enemy, if an army gets too far into enemy territory too fast it runs out of very necessary articles for that army. The Germans discovered that the hard way in the Battle of the Bulge. The old saying that an army marches on its stomach came from either Frederick the Great or Napoleon, two great leaders who understood that armies can't continue to fight if they can't be fed, have no place to stay, have no boots to march in or heavy winter clothing for facing a Russian winter.

The army may move slower because of all that "baggage", but it is *necessary* baggage. Some of those "impedimenta" in Caesar's day were things like swords and shields and helmets and shoes and breastplates. Does that list sound familiar? It should—it's the armor of God mentioned in Ephesians 6. It was hard for an ancient army to wage war without a shield to protect men from fiery darts or a sword to wield when they went on the offensive.

Some Christians feel that they are impeded in their fight against Satan. They may think of their children or their spouse or their own needs as things that "slow them down", but God has ordained that we fight best when we understand that to fight well we must have training, a base from which to operate, and the meeting of basic needs so we remain healthy and strong for the long haul. Marriage and parenthood prepare us for battle. The Bible even says we are blessed when we have a quiver full of children so we can fight better. (Psalm 127) Our own need for spiritual food and our need to provide for our families is not a hindrance to spiritual war-fare, it is the impedimenta necessary to wage war successfully.

Well Taught

Yesterday for Mother's Day the men of our church cooked breakfast for the community before church, as is our custom. There was a visiting family there who had been to our church previously, but they now live down state. The father of five and his four oldest, all freckle-faced boys, came early with one of our men to help with the breakfast. I wish you could have met these fine young men, ranging in age from about six to eleven.

I had to prepare the roses for distribution at our morning service, and asked if they could help. I figured that keeping them busy would keep them out of mischief. I'm sure on later reflection no mischief would have come from these well-trained youngsters. They jumped in to cut the flowers and place them in water picks, obviously taught to lend a helping hand with gusto to whatever project was on the agenda for the day. They are being raised on a ranch where they work cattle and I'm sure are used to working hard each day with chores.

I happened to also be their Sunday school teacher as we finished breakfast a bit later, and again I was struck by their openness, the eagerness and honesty in their faces, their ability to focus on the lesson, their knowledge of Scripture, and their polite behavior. It was more and more obvious as the morning wore on that they were being taught well by diligent parents. One incident happened just before Sunday school that was enlightening. The boys' father, a respectful, quiet man who was a wonderful example to them of service (jumping in himself to help cook breakfast), told one of the boys to go in to the bathroom and tuck his shirt in. I glanced down and a bit of the shirt was hanging out, and I thought to myself, *It all begins with small details, like making sure your shirt is tucked in.*

As much of our society dissolves before our eyes into anarchy and chaos, we see signs of disrespect everywhere. Seems very few in our popular culture have any respect for the police anymore, and they aren't trying to hide their rebellion toward their authority. Thousands of anarchists across the nation have torched businesses and even police stations, looted stores, hurt and intimidated others, and even committed murder, and the society as a whole seems unable to find the will to stop them. Our mainstream media and our politicians have been complicit in this, and in fact in many cases have encouraged it. But there is hope for the future in families that teach their sons to live in a godly manner. The young men I met showed respect for me (a stranger who asked them to help with a project), the women of the church (they eagerly wanted to help pass out roses at the end of the Mother's Day service), the other students in the Sunday school class, and each other.

And part of the secret is a father and mother who love each other (I sat next to them and visited during breakfast and they were holding hands) and who love and honor Christ. They are purposeful about raising their children in the nurture and admonition of the Lord, and so diligent about their training that they insist on shirts being tucked in as a sign of both self-respect and respect for others. God bless them and may their tribe increase all across our needy land!

Chapter Seven—Gotta Love Your Family

What's Right in America

I had the pleasure of being invited to the Texas Junior Braunvieh Association state show recently, and came away impressed with the cattle and the people. Fathers and mothers and mentors were there alongside the young men and women who showed the judges their heifers, and it is amazing (and not really surprising) what impact that has on the young people themselves. These young people are very familiar with hard work, intense competition, and the rewards of both. A number of them won belt buckles, banners, jackets, and money for college or for putting back into their cattle-raising operation. They understand that hard work and patience pay off in the end.

In addition to showcasing their cattle, youngsters from seven to twenty-one years old competed in speaking events, a quiz bowl where they identified certain paraphernalia used in the cattle industry, written and photo contests, and other tests of their skills and preparation. It was obvious they had spent a great deal of time preparing for the weekend's activities.

As I watched the hustle and bustle and interactions between young people and adults, I was reminded of young people's need for guidance and something productive to do. As young people were training their animals to follow them into the show ring and be judged, I realized that the parents and mentors of these youth were training the students to follow as well. I thought how different these kids were than the spoiled and out-of-control young adults you see on TV every night, "protesting" the greatest nation in the history of the world. It's an extremely safe bet that these youth will not be burning down their local Wendy's, or being carted away in handcuffs by the local police. When you teach a young child to work hard, to be engaged in healthy activities, and to live life in the right way, that youngster is set on the road to success instead of the road to anarchy.

Unsurprisingly, this is exactly God's design for family; dads and moms involved in the lives of their children, teaching them how to be successful, and more than just modeling values, they make sure their children are trained to *respect and follow* those values. And then there are the mentor adults who support and give time and money and resources to help kids grow up to be salt-of-the-earth citizens. Many of these folks long ago raised their own families, but here they are volunteering their time to invest in young lives. One friend of mine has been active in prison ministry for years, and he told me that he wants to spend more time helping kids become the kind of adults that won't end up in prison in the first place, believing the old adage "An ounce of prevention is worth a pound of cure."[97] Ben Franklin's witticism of 1736 still holds true today.

It's too bad CNN, ABC, and Fox News weren't there to cover this wonderful story. As we know, journalists aren't really in the news business; they are in the bad news business. Sorry, at this show there wasn't bad news, just an illustration of what makes America great. It's good to know this side of America; we see enough of the bad every day on our TV screens.

Woman Power

Yesterday was Father's Day, and in my sermon I talked about the most important thing in the life of a man and how wives are uniquely positioned to impact the behavior of a husband. We know from Ephesians 5 that the great need of a man is to command respect. We know that because wives are commanded to give their husbands respect, both at the beginning of the section on husband-wife relationships (5:22) and at the end of the section (5:33). Men will sacrifice, work hard, give their best at work because they want the respect of others; want to be known as a guy who is competent, who is "a hand". Men will sometimes move heaven and earth to be respected, which is why they often are so competitive.

But too often those same men who will give leadership and work so hard at their jobs will come home and fail to give leadership or do the hard work of leading their families. Why do men so often refuse to lead in the home?

There may be many reasons, but one key to unlocking a man's desire to give spiritual leadership in the home is the response of his wife in his efforts to lead. Leading is hard. By nature when you lead you become a target for criticism. And sadly, for most men, it doesn't take much criticism from the woman they love for them to conclude that they aren't good spiritual leaders, and men very naturally don't want to engage in activities where they feel inadequate. So for many men it takes very little pushback from a wife for them to just give up and not even try.

Men are powerful, but women are endowed with much power as well. A word of praise and respect from a wife can do wonders for a man. Dr. Laura Schlesinger tells of a young woman who understood this principle, and when her husband helped her open a jar of pickles she showed admiration for his strong muscles, and the man immediately dropped to the ground and did 30 push-ups.[98] With his actions he was saying, "You think that was something? You ain't seen the half of it!" He responded to her admiration by wanting to do more.

It's in a man's DNA to strive for respect, and when he gets it from the woman he loves he works harder to keep that respect. When a wife lets her husband know that she appreciates his leadership, it spurs him on to give more leadership. I saw an amazing comment from a former student posted to Facebook that is one wife's summation of her husband's leadership while on a recent vacation:

> *"He made my coffee for me every day of vacation. He pumped the gas, washed the windshield, found our hotels and went through the check-in/out process. He danced with me at a wedding and played with his boy in the ocean. He held my hand and sang along to all our road-tripping songs. He's the glue that holds us together. My knight in shining armor. The answer to all my prayers."*

What man wouldn't want to hear that from the woman he loves? What man wouldn't give all he has to keep that kind of respect? Men may be big and strong, but the woman's words, they have real power. Use those words well, ladies. Your man will step up to fulfill them.

Why Did God Make Me This Way?

This was a thought by my oldest daughter Rachel that was too good not to share. It is about her sister Laura, who has Down syndrome.

"Why did God make me this way? I didn't ask to be born with Down syndrome!" With tears in her eyes, my younger sister, Laura, demanded an explanation from my perplexed mother. Laura was in her early twenties and had always been treated simply as another member of the family. It had never occurred to her that there might be something special or different about her. She wasn't sure what Down syndrome was or what it might mean to her future, but a friend at the Functional Living Center had informed her that she "had it" and now she was devastated.

Her question, though new to her, was not a new one. It is a question many have asked in one way or another. *Why does God allow or cause or create people with limitations and special needs? Why does God make people who are very 'limited' or 'simple' or 'less' in certain ways? Why would a God with such power and wisdom, who is so limitless and perfect, intentionally create humanity that is none of those things? What quality-of-life does a person with 'limitations' really have? Would God really want people—'like that'—to exist?*

It is easy for us to see the hand of God at work in the mighty, the glorious, the grandiose, and the extraordinary. Since God is so great, it stands to reason that His handiwork would display awe-inspiring greatness. In fact, we almost make it a conditional requirement—"*if* God is so great, He will only and always reveal Himself in ways and in people that I deem 'impressive.'"

The problem is, we fundamentally misunderstand the nature and the character of God. He doesn't have anything to prove. He is not like us—insecure and unsure—in need of the approval of others. He is not tainted by pride nor is He driven by a desire to impress anyone. He does what He pleases. He creates simply for the joy of it and because it reveals aspects of Himself to those who behold it. He isn't threatened or diminished by giving His image to those we might describe as "less" in some way. In fact, in many ways, they are more perfectly suited to exhibit His true nature.

In our arrogance, we like the idea that our worth can be earned because then we would have reason to boast. The problem is that if you can earn it, then you can also lose it. And if you can lose it, then you have to work to maintain it. This is why pride is not only a sin and an abomination before the Lord, but it is really a yoke of bondage. One of Laura's characteristic traits is that she is totally unassuming. There is an innocence and openness that is without pretense. Completely comfortable in her own skin, she is simply herself in every situation without regard to anyone or anything that is going on around her. She has no awareness of status or rank nor is she concerned with impressing others or making a name for herself. Her lack of inhibitions produces everything from unconventional wardrobe choices to impromptu speeches full of hilarious non-sequiturs to spontaneous tap dancing (with or without music). In her childlike simplicity, she demonstrates a profound truth—the truest freedom is found in humility.

This is an attribute of God that we often overlook. The almighty, all-sufficient, incomparable, omnipotent and infinite Creator—the One who defies description in His majesty—is at the same time completely pure, guileless, and humble. It is He who delights in using "foolish things to confound the wise" (1 Corinthians 1:27). It is He who made Himself "a little lower than the angels" (Hebrews 2:9) in order to redeem rebellious, fallen mankind. It is He who, in His humanity, "did not consider equality with God a thing to be grasped but humbled himself even to death on a cross" (Philippians 2:8).

Years ago, I experienced two miscarried pregnancies. Both were discovered at the first doctor's visit when no heartbeat could be detected. In one case, the doctor estimated that the baby had lived a few days. In the other, he speculated it had survived only a few hours. I have wondered from time to time why God would go to the effort to create children whose time here was so brief. I have wondered if I will recognize these babies in heaven and if I will better be able to understand what glory God gained from their short lives.

The problem is that my premise is flawed. I am making the assumption that God's name and His glory and His likeness is somehow tied to human achievement or what we can produce. He delights and glories in our *existence,* not in our achievement. Anything we might accomplish is really HIS accomplishment anyway. What better way to demonstrate the value He places on human life than to include babies and people who do nothing and achieve nothing but simply exist for a short time and then go to be with Him? So frequently we look with pity on those who have less in one way or another. However, the reality is that those with less often live more abundantly than those weighed down with more. It's easy to be so consumed with myself and my own image that I forget God created me to reflect His image. On the other hand, the less of me that is put forward, the more God Himself can be on display.

I am so grateful that God sees fit to send people like Laura into our lives. We need to be delivered from the bondage of self-glorification and the pressure of performance. We need to see the glory in humility, the wonder of simplicity, and the virtue of innocence. Matthew 5:8 tells us that the pure in heart shall see God. It is wonderful to realize that the pure in heart allow the rest of us to see Him as well! How can we know the beauty of simplicity if it is never on display? How can we appreciate the joy of innocence without witnessing it? Without "the least of these", how would we ever experience the refreshment of humility in a world so polluted by pride?

Chapter Seven—Gotta Love Your Family

Laura with younger sisters Deborah, Lydia, and Hannah

The Most Important Legacy

When I was young I realized that I wanted to leave a legacy when I passed from this life. Even in junior high school, when nobody around me would have suspected it, I thought about becoming a good husband and good father, and I wondered what it would take to get there. As I got older and made my way through high school and college, I listened carefully when a pastor, youth pastor, or other speaker talked about developing character that is worthy of emulation, and I slowly grew in my spiritual development.

When I met my future wife, Gwynne, I had grown much, but I still had a long, long, way to go. We dated and eventually married, and I had a chance to try out all the lessons I had learned by reading and hearing great speakers over the years. I learned, as everyone does, that it is one thing to read or listen, quite another to put into practice what you have read or heard. I failed many times. But I was still willing to grow and learn. Gwynne was too. Early in our marriage she began an extensive study concerning the Bible's message on children. The study took her five years to complete, but one of the first things she discovered was that God sent children as blessings into the lives of parents and the larger community, and that we should welcome each child as from His hand. We prayed about it and decided to give our family planning over to the Lord. We told Him we would receive any children He sent our way. I had been told years earlier by a doctor that I might not be able to be a father, and, interestingly, Gwynne had also been told by a different doctor that she might not ever be a mother. I sure wish we could go back and find those doctors and introduce them to our eleven children!

In a sense Gwynne and I realized how counter-culture we were with this decision about accepting as many children as God would send, and we knew in some fundamental ways how much it would affect every area of our lives from then on, but we could not have known the entire story at the time. It had to be played out slowly, month by month and year by year. As each new child came along we endured the jokes and ribbing and criticism from the larger community—much of it the Christian community. "Bruce, do you know what causes that?" "Don't you have enough already?" "Are you guys ever gonna stop having kids?" "Quick, look at Mrs. Howard, she's not pregnant." We heard it all. People didn't know what to think or say about this huge family. We definitely were not going to sneak up on anybody. When the Howards showed up people always knew it!

And here Gwynne and I are on the other side, in our sixties, our children grown. Our youngest just turned 18 and graduates high school this year. At 66-years-old I'll finally have all of them through the first thirteen grades. And from this side of the decision, if I had it to do all over again, would I change anything?

Not at all. I have always been a competitive person, and wanted to win whether it was a pick-up game of basketball or a game of checkers. And I carried that competitive spirit into my years of coaching, first in athletics, and then for 27 years in UIL Science competitions. Those years were good to me and helped me grow as a teacher and leader. My students won numerous medals, plaques, and accolades, and I'm proud of our accomplishments together.

But near the end of my teaching career, and certainly now in retirement from teaching, I have a new appreciation for what really matters in life. All the plaques and trophies and medals and ribbons pale in comparison to the significance of Christ...and family. Recently our daughter Laura turned 29, and we had a party for her attended by most of her siblings and most of our grandchildren. As we sat in a large circle and shared what we appreciated most about Laura (a family tradition at birthday gatherings), I realized yet again that when it comes down to it, these people, so dear to me, part of my own soul, are the most important part of a legacy. I suppose a legacy is simply something you leave behind for the following generations, and so it is fitting that they, a product of my marriage and my teaching, are by definition a legacy, and the one that counts most. One day I will pass, but something of me will be left behind. That something is embodied in my children and grandchildren, and I realize that the Lord has been so good to Gwynne and me, giving us such a large quiver full of children (Psalm 127). Truly at this point in my life I am not ashamed to stand in the gate with my family, for they fill me with pride. I am the richest of men, for the Lord has loaned me a growing number of souls that will impact the world for Him. It's true that you can't take it with you when you die. But you can sure leave something worthwhile behind. I am grateful to a wife who saw before I did that the most worthwhile things in life aren't things at all, or accomplishments either, but souls that last for eternity.

The Howard family in 2007

Chapter Eight— The Church

I have spent my whole life in the church, and always felt comfortable there. The church has its warts and faults to be sure, for the church is made of people. But those people are the Bride of Christ, and He dearly loves them and calls them His own. We as believers must be committed to the purity and growth of its members. I have been a children's pastor, youth pastor, and senior pastor for all of my adult life, and am as committed as ever to helping the church prepare for the Lord to come and get her. And, as the apostle John once wrote, "I have no greater joy than to hear that my children [in the faith] walk in truth (III John 4)." The church is the best place to raise children, for it is there that our family values are validated and magnified by others. It is there that they meet others who are seeking God and trying their best to honor Him. It is there that they meet all kinds of different people, and learn to get along with them and love them, even those who are quirky. It is in the church and because of the church that my children understand the discipline of getting up and getting ready, being quiet for a while, listening intently to another as they teach, showing respect for elders, and being an example to those who are younger. Yes, the church has her problems, because the church is made of people. But the Lord hasn't given up on her yet, and neither should we.

A Biblical Philosophy

Colossians 2:8 warns us to not be tricked by vain philosophy. Everyone is a philosopher. It just depends on whether your philosophy is based on a solid foundation or not. What does a viable *biblical* philosophy look like?

1) It starts with a firm conviction that Word of God is completely true, and is the ultimate guide for understanding God, the world, and man's place in it.
   a) Psalm 12:6-7—The words of the Lord are pure words
   b) Psalm 119:89—Forever O Lord, Your Word is settled
   c) Psalm 119:105—Thy Word is a lamp unto my feet
   d) Psalm 119:160—The entirety of Your Word is truth
   e) Hebrews 4:12—The Word of God is living and active and a discerner of thoughts and intents. To know myself I must know it.
   f) James 1:22-25—I must do the Word to be blessed. It's the only way I can know what to do and what to be in this world.
2) So since the underlying presupposition of life is that God's Word is true and reliable, what do I know about God?
   a) He is omniscient, omnipresent, and omnipotent (He knows everything, is everywhere, and can do anything)—Psalm 139
   b) He is light, in Him is no darkness—I John 1:5
   c) He is love, so everything He does is because He loves—I John 4:7-8
   d) He is perfectly faithful, perfectly merciful, and perfectly reliable—I Corinthians 1:9
   e) He is perfectly holy—I Peter 1:16
   f) He can become angry, and He is judge of all the earth—Psalm 75:7

g) He is triune, always consistent, receives sinners, binds up the broken-hearted, heals the sick, and is a Savior. He is everything His Word declares Him to be.
3) What do I know about God's Son, Jesus Christ?
　　a) He is the image of the invisible God—Colossians 1:15
　　b) He is my Creator—John 1:1-3
　　c) He is my Redeemer—Galatians 3:13
　　d) His death took away my sin and His resurrection proved that He was who He claimed to be—I Peter 2:24
4) In light of who God is and what Jesus came to do, what do I know about myself and my place in the world?
　　a) I am a sinner—Romans 3:23
　　b) In my flesh dwells no good thing—Romans 8:7-8
　　c) I deserve eternal death because of my sin—Romans 6:23a
　　d) I can know Christ and have eternal life—Romans 6:23b and John 17:3
　　e) I am bought with a price and am not my own—I Corinthians 6:19-20
　　　 My time is not my own, my things are not my own, my money is not my own, and my talents are not my own.
　　f) Because God made Jesus to be sin on my behalf, I am a new creation in Christ. Old things have passed away and all are made new in Him. 2 Corinthians 5:17-21

Therefore my purpose in life is to glorify God in everything I do. I must study to show myself approved, fill my life with God's Word in order to keep on the right path, listen to the Holy Spirit who guides me, pray without ceasing, give thanks in everything, walk in authority over Satan, be involved in good works to the glory of God, attend a Bible-believing church and serve faithfully in it, and point others to Him for salvation and purpose by bringing people to Christ and mentoring them.

Jesus said we all are going to build our houses on something, either rock or sand (Matthew 7). The storms of life are going to come, the rain and wind will do their best to level each house. He said we were wise if we built our houses on the rock of His words. Then they will stand, because they are connected to something solid. Paul told us that Christ was the best foundation we could lay for our understanding of our meaning on this earth. (I Corinthians 3:11) I couldn't agree more.

A Picture of the Church

In mid-September 1940, at 10:03 p.m., U-boat 48, commanded by Heinrich Bleichrodt, fired a torpedo at the *City of Benares*, which was traveling in a convoy headed for Canada. The torpedo ran true, exploded, and the ship sank in 31 minutes. Some of the 406 passengers and crew died instantly; some died as they were trying to lower lifeboats and rafts. The North Atlantic was very unforgiving.

But nearly 300 made it to the lifeboats in the storm-tossed seas, and began a harrowing night trying to survive the wind, waves, and sleet battering them. What made this situation rather unique was that 90 of the passengers were English children, ages five to fifteen, on their way to North America to escape the Luftwaffe's bombing of their mother country. Their parents had sent them away, praying this act would insure their survival during the awful war raging around them.

Many souls perished that night on the wild ocean. The winds increased to 50 miles per hour, the waves overturned some of the lifeboats. Other boats were full of water that covered victims and caused hypothermia. Some lifeboat passengers were washed overboard and perished that way.

But some made it through the night and all through the next day to be saved. The heroes were many. Hugh Crofton Simms, commander of the British destroyer HMS *Hurricane*, pushed his ship at almost reckless speed over 300 miles to come to the rescue. One of his sailors, Albert Gorman, took the destroyer's whaleboat out time and again and rescued some. Another, George Pound, took a 20-foot dive off the Hurricane to rescue a woman who was drowning. In one lifeboat several survivors owed their lives to others.

10-year-old Derek Bech was alive because his mother Marguerite had covered him during the ordeal with her body, keeping him warm enough to survive. Marguerite herself had been at the point of giving up and dying when her daughter Sonia begged her to renew her hope of rescue. Sonia was alive only because as a wave had thrown her out of her craft a strong sailor named Tommy Milligan pulled her back aboard. Milligan and the Bechs had Eric Davis (a BBC correspondent) to thank, for he had alerted them to their danger on the ship and had gotten them to a life raft on time. They barely got off the ship before it sunk. And none of them would have made it had not they been pre-rescued by second officer Leslie Lewis—whose own ship the *Marina* had also been sunk—who had erected a sail on his lifeboat and found them with their raft breaking up. Had he not plucked them from the sea when he did they wouldn't have been alive an hour later.

Two teenage English girls kept each other alive. Their lifeboat had been overturned shortly after it pulled away from the liner, and they had clung to the keel for over 18 hours before they were rescued. Beth Cummings and Bess Walder should have died of exposure, but they hung on together, because they realized that if one of them gave up and was lost, the other would die as well. It was their constant encouragement of one another that both later attributed to their survival.[99]

How the church must be like this; filled with men, women, and children who think about others, who care for others, who engage in rescuing others from disaster, who encourage others to hang on and not give in to despair. The times in which we live are not unique in world history; there have been many times believers have suffered with the world around them chaotic and dangerous. But in every situation, believers should answer the call to encourage one another, and all the more, as we see the Day approaching (Hebrews 10:25). Over 100 souls were saved from the sinking of the *City of Benares,* souls that helped one another hang on until their final rescue was complete. Let us, the church, encourage one another to hang on as well.

A Picture of the Church (Part II)

I shared the story of the disaster and rescue of passengers from the *City of Benares* in 1940. Over 100 people were pulled from the North Atlantic by seamen from the HMS *Hurricane*, and there were many heroes in the story.

But as Paul Harvey used to say, there is a *"rest of the story."* As evening fell during the rescue, the captain of the *Hurricane* worried whether he had found all the lifeboats. He hadn't. Lifeboat 12 was a victim of its own good fortune—it had been lowered properly, wasn't damaged or filled with water, and so it moved through the water much faster than the other vessels floating that awful night. When rescue came for the others Lifeboat 12 had moved well beyond the search area of the *Hurricane*.

To add to their troubles, the boat, designed for a maximum of 40 souls, contained 46 people. The "skipper" of the boat, Seaman Ronnie Cooper, had helped drag eight people from the water, saving their lives but causing additional stress on the others in the boat. Now food and water would have to be shared among more people.

In literature of the time, preparing people to survive in lifeboats, the problems people had to fight were pictured as demons called "Fear", "Anxiety", "Loss of Faith", "Anger", and "Fatigue". Authorities knew that the biggest enemies of survivors was not the lack of food or water or shelter from the elements, but those inner things that could disrupt the harmony and mental stability of those forced to live together in stressful circumstances.

Again, we can see how this relates to the church. The church is made of those who are trying to live their lives as best they can, and in sometimes stressful circumstances they must get along with one another to fight common enemies. Fear, loss of faith, anger, and fatigue attack members of the church, and those things are demons that work against the harmony and goodwill of church members. Aboard Lifeboat 12 the crowded men, children, and one woman were forced to deal with their own fears and anxieties without causing panic among the others. Mary Cornish, the lone woman on board, survived because she had to care for the six evacuee children they had in the boat, boys ranging from nine to thirteen years of age.[100]

More than half the men were from India, employees of the Benares. Many of them could barely speak English. Then there was Harry Peard. A sailor from the *Benares*, he had an unconquerable spirit, was an incurable optimist, with boundless energy and one big setback—he was relationally obtuse. He berated Miss Cornish on her handling of the boys, criticized Seaman Cooper, irritated Father O'Sullivan the priest and the Pole, Bohdan Nagorski. He used crude language and almost caused a mutiny among the Indians. But, when it was all said and done, in the eight days the boat was at sea, when the chips were down, he was credited with keeping hope alive and infusing optimism in the others at a time when they were ready to give up and die. Several of the survivors said that had he not been aboard, they would have given up and perished.[101]

The church is on journey together. We are kept together by a common faith, and by common enemies. We exist to rescue others in peril, even though it works against our own ease. We are people of diverse races, backgrounds, understandings, and temperaments. And we have people in our midst who have trouble getting along with others, but in their turn prove themselves valuable members of our community. We should always keep in mind that our enemies are not each other; neither is our biggest enemy the circumstances we are in. We each fight a battle within ourselves to conquer those attitudes and character flaws that may be the undoing of the entire enterprise. We are accountable to our Captain and to each other to win these battles and minister to one another on our collective journey.

Play Your Position

When people watch a football game, most of them focus on and identify with the playmakers—the quarterbacks, running backs, and split ends on offense—the guys who get to score the touchdowns and dance in the end zone. Or they might identify with the playmakers on defense—the cornerbacks and safeties who make touchdown-saving tackles or interceptions—the Neon Deion Sanders of the defense who attract the attention.

But there is a football truism that works for every level of the game. What wins games in Pee-Wee football, high school football, college football, and even pro football is not necessarily the quality of the skill players, but the quality of the linemen. If you have good linemen you can run the football, and as football coaches understand, if you can run the football you can win lots of football games. No matter how good the quarterback or running back is, they are going nowhere if the line doesn't do its job and block for them.

Conversely, how do you control the game on the defensive side of the ball? Your linemen stop the run. Those guards and tackles and defensive ends have to do their job because if the only stops are made by linebackers, cornerbacks, and safeties five yards or more down the field, your team can't get the other team off the field. They will rack up first down after first down and use up precious clock time while doing so. So here is praise for the linemen of the game! They are the heart of the team, and without good ones who do their job there will be few victories.

Now what in the world does that have to do with you? You don't play football. No, but you are on a team called the church. And there is a tendency for people outside the church to admire the folks on stage, the "skill" players, the "platform personalities" who get to sing and speak in front of everyone. Everyone's eyes are on them. But what if you are "just" a person in the pew who doesn't get up on stage very often, if ever? Then you are a lineman. But you are the most important part of the team. You don't have a glamorous job, but you have the most important job.

Without you doing your job, the church has few victories. Don't ever get discouraged over the job God gives you to do. Remember, "God has set the members, each one of them, in the body just as He pleased." (I Corinthians 12:18) Play your position well, and watch the whole church rejoice in the wins that pile up!

Power Outage

Recently a large swathe of the Texas panhandle had no electricity for several hours as an unusually strong October "winter" storm hit the area. Every time we lose power like this it seems to take us back into simpler (and more difficult) times. Much of our home is powered by electricity, but fortunately we have a propane tank and heater and a gas stove, so we during the outage we could stay relatively warm and heat water for bathing and washing dishes. And fortunately the hard-working men and women of the power company got us going again fairly quickly. It wasn't too many years ago that we were out of power for days instead of hours.

Life is hard without power. You move from efficiency and accomplishment to survival quickly. You take away people's TV watching and you find out what they're really made of. I wouldn't exactly call it the Stone Age, but things are different when you turn all the lights out. Habits persist though. How many times did I walk into the bathroom or bedroom and flip on the light switch, only to be reminded that life, at least briefly, was not the same anymore?

If we are going to do more than survive we too must have a power source, from within. Without a source of power we will find ourselves groping in the dark, losing warmth and a sense of purpose. We become listless and hunker down hoping someone will come to the rescue. There is a Source of power for the inner man, and the apostle Paul was plugged into it. In 2nd Corinthians he was extremely candid about the hardships he had faced in his life. In the first few chapters he used words like afflicted, despair, persecution, suffering, anguish, hard-pressed, perplexed, and struck down. He was not deceptive about the difficulty of life. But he tells us in 4:16 that "Even though our outward man is perishing, yet the inward man is being renewed day by day." How does a person who experienced all those privations continue to be renewed so that they can face the challenges of each day? They have an inner power source. The inner light is still on because they are plugged into an outer source. I could plug my lamp into the wall socket at my house as much as I wanted during the blackout, but until the power company got the lines up and running again it was all for naught. Thankfully the Source of our inner strength never has a downed power line.

"Abide in Me", He said (John 15:4). If you do, He promised a never-ending source of Life for producing the fruit that glorifies God. If you fail to abide no permanent fruit can ever be created, for He also said "... apart from Me you can do nothing." (John 15:5) If there is no power coming to the inner man, all you end up doing is thrashing around in the dark.

Praying For You

Recently I had to make a hurried trip to Kansas City; a long journey that is tiresome in the best of circumstances. And the reason for my journey was to help resolve a stressful family matter. The expedition had a number of potential stressors, and on one hand I looked on it with a certain amount of foreboding. On the other, it was necessary, and so, like facing surgery or some other unenviable situation, I was ready to get the trip and the task behind me.

What actually transpired reminded me again of the power of intercessory prayer and the importance of having a church family. I knew that many family members (church and physical family too) were praying for me, and there was a palpable peace and strength during my 550-mile drive. Upon arriving late in the evening I felt refreshed and ready for the task at hand the next day. Awakened at 4:30 the next morning, I should have been exhausted, but instead had a wonderful time of Bible study and prayer in preparation for the assignment I had before me that day.

Chapter Eight—The Church

The Lord orchestrated all to satisfaction, and I was able to return home by late that evening. 1100 miles of driving, alone, in less than 36 hours, and an unwelcome duty brought to completion. The great thing about it all was the peace, joy, and power of knowing that God was in control and the Giver of enabling grace. People praying make a difference!

Never take lightly the ministry of interceding for others. Who knows how many people are still alive because you've prayed for God to heal them of their cancer, or extend their lives? Who knows how many have come to salvation because God has answered your heartfelt prayers for them? Who knows what amazing grace has been shown to and through the saints of God because you've lifted them up during their time of testing? Check out the epistles of Paul. In nearly every one of them he mentions that he is praying for those to whom he writes, or he appreciates their prayers for him, or both. For example, in writing to the Romans he says he unceasingly lifts them up in prayer, and indicates that part of that prayer is to be able to come to see them. The implication is that though he has been hindered from coming to them (Romans 1:13), between his own prayers and the prayers of the Roman Christians, perhaps God will sanction the trip.

How easy it is to say casually to a friend or family member, "I'll pray for you." Don't treat it casually though. Lift them up before the throne of heaven. You have ready access through Christ to the place to find "help in time of need." (Hebrews 4:16) Avail yourself of that privilege. Others are counting on you to aid them in their stressful journey through life. It certainly made a difference for me in my adventure last week, turning an unpleasant task into an illustration of God's sustaining help and favor.

Surprise Attack?

The Japanese attack on Pearl Harbor December 7, 1941 followed a detailed, elaborate, and crafty plan that caught the U.S. fleet completely by surprise. But it shouldn't have been that way.

In January 1932 the U.S. Naval Planning Board conducted a mock attack at Pearl that used the exact same tactics that would prove so effective 9 years later. Two aircraft carriers, the Saratoga and the Lexington, sailed through thick weather that masked their movements and released 152 airplanes for the mock attack on Sunday, February 7th. Sunday at dawn was chosen for the raid because it was assumed that the guard would be lowest on that particular day of the week and at that particular time of day. The fighter planes "knocked out" the planes on the ground and the bombers "sank" all the hypothetical vessels in the harbor.

Some high-ranking officers wanted to revise the entire organization of the navy to prevent such a disaster from actually occurring, but Washington refused to take decisive action.

In Tokyo things were different. Thanks to a network of spies, most notably Takeo Yoshikawa, who had been living in Hawaii for months collecting detailed information of the war games, the U.S. response was sent to Japan, and the Japanese realized they had been given a wonderful gift by the very nation they wanted to destroy. With only minor modifications this plan was executed to perfection on that "Day that will live in infamy." Thankfully for world history the "sleeping giant" awoke in time to help defeat both Nazi Germany and the empire of Japan as well. No nation except America was capable of winning two wars at once.[102]

Today America is under attack again, and the patterns between our present situation and 1941 are similar. We have an enemy (Satan) that has a plan. He has been watching us carefully, making note of our weaknesses. He realizes that even though we have seen the results of the past, we have not taken decisive action against them, and so he can surprise us again. Marxists have told us for decades their agenda; to destroy the nuclear family, to set Americans at each others' throats, to indoctrinate young people with false history and misinformation, to align the elites of the media, the entertainment industry, and the political class against the middle class. And while we are sleeping and ignoring their plans, the ambush begins.

Perhaps the sleeping giant has been awakened again. We are seeing conservative Christian voices being raised in protest to the anarchists. Perhaps once again God will awaken America before the world erupts in flames. Let us pray that is the case. On Sunday morning December 7th, 1941, sailors slept while their enemy closed in. Let us hope that we will arouse from our slumber in time. Why in the world are we surprised that Satan uses these familiar tactics again? After all, they've worked before.

That's What It's All About

One of my friends named Richard is a prayer warrior, and he is focused like a laser beam on seeing people come to Christ. He often makes the remark when kids come back from camp and have made decisions for Christ for baptism or to surrender to God's call on their lives, "that's what it's all about." And he's right. The church exists to glorify God and grow in the faith, and to share the gospel with the people around them, so to fulfill the Great Commission given them by the Lord they must lead others to Christ and baptize them in the name of the Father, Son, and Holy Spirit, then disciple them.

At our church we often pray for students in our church and community, and it is sure exciting when we see a harvest. We've had that lately at both kids' camp and youth camp. A number of young people have been touched by the Lord, and we are setting up baptismal services for them. Others have surrendered to God's call on their lives to step up as leaders to share the gospel with others. One of our young men will be preaching at a nearby church next week while the pastor is gone. He led one of our church group times during youth camp and did a fantastic job. Another camper from our group is only going into the 7th grade, but she volunteered to lead a church group discussion, and did a wonderful job as well. Another of our campers wants to use his musical talents to become a worship leader some day (he already helps lead the praise at his church, so he's got a good head start).

Harvest time! It's an exciting time. It's a time where we see the effective, fervent prayers of righteous people avail much, touching lives and making a difference for the kingdom of God. It is the church being the church, with elders praying for and guiding young people to give their lives to the Lord. What a difference it will make in their decisions and the trajectory of their lives. It's fun to see the church make a difference in young people, and to hope that they will be the spiritual leaders our country needs to bring America back to the Lord. And as Richard says, *"that's what it's all about!"*

Watch Out for Copperheads

During the Civil War northern Democrats who had sympathies with the Confederacy were called Copperheads. The name came from a lapel pin made by open advocates of the group by cutting out the Liberty head from large copper pennies of the day and wearing it as an ornament. The name also implied rather brazenly that the members of the group, like copperhead snakes, would lie in wait to strike when the opportunity arose. They advocated peace at any price, detested Abraham Lincoln, and wanted the South to be free to secede.

When two of their leaders, Samuel "Sunset" Cox and Clement Vallandigham embarked on a scheme to upset the balance of power in the Congress through parliamentarian shenanigans, Lincoln was understandably irritated at them both, but especially at Vallandigham, the man who he called a "wily agitator." Lincoln had sent Vallandigham south to the rebel capitol of Richmond earlier in the year, hoping to be rid of him. Lincoln was trying desperately to hold the Union together, giving his very heart and soul to see the nation united again, but there were opponents who constantly made this work infinitely harder.[103]

In the local church there are sometimes those who work against unity in the body of Christ as well. The apostle Paul actually calls some of them out by name when he writes to Timothy with instructions on being a church pastor. It apparently was Martin Luther who first noted that whenever God builds a church, the devil will build a chapel near it. There often are those who, like snakes in the grass, lie in wait to strike at the heart of the unity Christ desires for His church.

Paul wanted the churches he started to be unified in the faith. So should we all. He said "I, therefore, the prisoner of the Lord, beseech you to walk worthy of the calling with which you were called, with all lowliness and gentleness, with longsuffering, bearing with one another in love, endeavoring to keep the unity of the Spirit in the bond of peace." (Ephesians 4:1-3) As far as it depends on you, pursue peace with all men. (Romans 12:18) But also be on the lookout for copperheads who seek to disrupt the true work of God in a local church.

Chapter Nine—
The Nature of God

You know of course that we are all theologians, for a theologian is simply somebody who has ideas about the nature of God. The question is not whether or not we *are* theologians, but whether or not we are *good* theologians. In my view good theologians are those who order their faith according to the plumb line of Scripture. Our understanding of God must come from there. And to some degree, every blog I've written for this book goes back to my thoughts about who God is and what He expects of us as His master creation. We owe Him no less than to give our lives contemplating the meaning of the universe from His perspective. Scripture indicates that the greatest thing in life is to know God, to appreciate His goodness, mercy, love, and justice. I'm not sure of everything we are going to do in heaven, but I feel confident that much of our time will be spent diving deep into God's matchless character. Knowing Him as He is will take eternity.

All Nature Sings

My wife, daughter, and I recently returned from a trip to West Virginia and Ohio. Coming from a dry and thirsty land the first thing that strikes you about these regions of our country is the effect that water has on plant life. For us a river might be 3 inches deep, or even just a dry riverbed. There when you talk about rivers you talk about the Ohio or Monongahela, rivers of depth and substance that are deep and flow all year long. And the trees! 50 and 60-feet tall or bigger, majestic hickories and maples and pines, trees that fill the valleys and the hills with their beauty, trees that remind you of the trees in Psalm 1, trees "planted by the rivers of water", trees that bring forth fruit in season, "whose leaf does not wither." Jeremiah says of these trees that they are "not worried about drought." (Jeremiah 17:8) And the lush, green grass we saw, thick and beautiful, covering the hills. Yes, it's amazing what a little rain can do for a place. When we flew back into Amarillo at the end of the week we couldn't help but notice the desert-like landscape.

We stayed at Blackwater Falls State Park in West Virginia during the first part of our trip, and our timing couldn't have been more perfect. We were there during the height of the fall foliage color change. I've never seen so many pretty shades of red, orange, yellow, and green all mixed together. It was breathtaking. And there were lots of folks there to enjoy and record the changing seasons of nature. Professional and semi-professional photographers were there in abundance, snapping away at the panorama around them; hikers of all sizes and shapes; family groups having a wonderful time together breathing in the beauty of the scenery around them.

And there's nothing wrong with that at all. It's part of why we were there, to soak our souls in the peace and quiet of the environment. And yet I wondered as I watched not only nature, but human nature, whether all those folks could see beyond the natural to the Creator behind it. Did the beauties of nature point them to the beauty of the One who made not only the trees and grass and rivers, but they themselves? Did they begin their day opening the Word of God and allowing Him to speak to them? Did they worship the God of nature, or just the nature itself? Hopefully all the folks we saw thought about the creativity and power of the Lord as they enjoyed the workings of His hand. Nature is good, but it is best when it reminds us of the wonderful God who made it and sustains it. We must appreciate it for what it is, and what it is not. It is not an end in itself, but a reminder that "This is my Father's world, and to my listening ears [and seeing eyes], all nature sings...the rocks and trees, the skies and seas, His hand the wonders wrought."[104] Last week that music was sweet indeed.

West Virginia beauty

Father Knows Best

Recently I heard a message that included the phrase "father knows best". If you're an old dog like me you remember the show of that title from the 1950's starring Robert Young and Jane Wyatt. The idea that father knows best is now parodied and mocked, but it certainly hasn't done our society any good to throw out the wisdom of a good father who actually leads his home in making good decisions.

The post-modern world has an inflated notion of its own ability to think clearly, and what has been the result? Progressive policies that are a disaster for the country; planned anarchy; waste of taxpayer monies more egregious than ever before; and a country so divided that many fear a second civil war.

The problem, according to the speaker, was that we as humans have too much EGO. Ego, he said, means to "Edge God Out." I thought this a clever acronym. We have failed to realize that we cannot make wise decisions without consulting the Book. Adam and Eve got in trouble when they thought their way was better than God's way, and their descendants have trooped along right behind them making the same poor decisions without learning from the disasters they create.

My favorite president, Abraham Lincoln, said it well. "We have been the recipients of the choicest bounties of Heaven. We have been preserved, these many years, in peace and prosperity. We have grown in numbers, wealth and power, as no other nation has ever grown. But we have forgotten God. We have forgotten the gracious hand which preserved us in peace, and multiplied and enriched and strengthened us; and we have vainly imagined, in the deceitfulness of our hearts, that all these blessings were produced by some superior wisdom and virtue of our own. Intoxicated with unbroken success, we have become too self-sufficient to feel the necessity of redeeming and preserving grace, too proud to pray to the God that made us!"[105]

Amen! He called for a national day of fasting so the nation could again turn to the God that made them, the God who had the answers for their problems, the God who was their only hope of national survival. We find ourselves in a national crisis again. Will we finally learn that Father knows best, or will we continue on thrashing about in national confusion while our country crumbles around us?

Fight of Faith

We are called believers. The implication is that the main characteristic we possess is belief in God, trust in His Word and ways. But so many believers are filled with doubt. Some doubt whether their sins are really forgiven. Others doubt that they are fit for heaven. Many believe that they really are cleansed from their sins and they are sure of their place in heaven, but they doubt whether God could ever use them in His service. They say they are doubting themselves, but all doubts reflect our view of God, our belief or unbelief in His ability to not only save, but to sanctify.

But imagine how foolish for a sheep to say, "I cannot believe the shepherd could really care about me since I sometimes wander off. Surely the shepherd cares mostly about the sheep who always do what they ought." How silly! If all sheep did exactly what they were supposed to do, the owner of the sheep could turn them out in the morning and say, "Y'all have a good time feeding in the pasture. Be sure you're home by six!" No shepherd would even be necessary. But we know that sheep need a shepherd in the worst way, because *all* of them will wander if not watched. The shepherd's job is to guide and care for all the sheep and keep them from danger. The wandering sheep is his job security.

Or imagine yet again that someone says, "The doctor can't care about me because I am sick. He can only take care of those who are well." The doctor's intense and expensive training prepares him to care for those who are sick. The healthy don't need a doctor. His entire career hinges on his ability and willingness to care for those in need and get them healthy again. So we see that our very *need* of shepherding, our very *requirement* of a doctor is our greatest *claim* to the love of God. Far from being the characteristic that disqualifies us for His care, our need is the greatest qualification we possess; in fact, the only qualification necessary.

Isaiah 66:1 tells us that heaven is God's throne, and the earth His footstool. In other words, God is above all things. But then verse 2 tells us God looks at the one who "is poor and of a contrite spirit, and who trembles at My word." No need for greatness when approaching the throne of the Most High. His heart is with the broken. David, in his beautiful psalm of penitence (Psalm 51), says "...a broken and a contrite heart—these, O God, You will not despise."

So, Christian, lay your doubts aside. God is big enough to take you, broken and weak as you are, and make of you one of the "saints who are on the earth. They are the excellent ones, in whom is all my delight." (Psalm 16:3) God made Jesus, who knew no sin, to become sin for us, that we might become the righteousness of God. (2nd Corinthians 5:21) It seems an unbelievable exchange, but God commands us to believe it and experience it.

Final Notice

I recently bought a new (2013) car. For the Howards, it qualifies as new if it has less than 65,000 miles on it. Anyway, it's bright red and runs well, and I like it a lot. I've only had the car for a couple of months, and already I've been bombarded with notices from the warranty department warning me that "YOU HAVE NOT CONTACTED US to get your service contract up-to-date." I'm sure you know the drill. Statistics tell us that more money is made in the finance department of a car dealership than anywhere else, so it's a lucrative thing for the dealer to push their product and use fear to do so.[106] They know that in the long run they will make more money on people buying extended warranties than they will outlay in expenses fixing those vehicles.[107]

In big bold highlighted words on the notice they tell you that you will be "FINANCIALLY LIABLE for all repairs to your vehicle" if you don't get the extended warranty. I was certainly amazed, blithely assuming that by purchasing the used vehicle they would naturally take care of all future expenses on the upkeep of my car since they sold it to me. "PLEASE CALL IMMEDIATELY", the flyer urges. They want you to know that this is "EXTREMELY URGENT AND TIME SENSITIVE", and that this is the "FINAL NOTICE."

I can only hope. You've received notices like this, haven't you? There are very few things for certain in this life besides the love of a redemptive God and the corruption of the U.S. Congress, but one added thing is the fact that this notice will definitely in no way be the final notice of my expiring warranty offer. I'm looking at the paper now, dated June 24, 2021. Since then I've had two pink cards and two other notices sent to me. That's four missives sent within three weeks *after* the "final notice" was mailed. Somehow I begin to doubt their word that this will be, indeed, the final notice.

But God doesn't work that way. His Word says that as long as today is called today we should respond to His notice. Indeed, it is EXTREMELY URGENT AND TIME SENSITIVE. He wants us to know that if we don't respond we will be LIABLE. He warns some that they have NOT CONTACTED Him about the liability they face, and He urges them to PLEASE CALL IMMEDIATELY. Thank God that He hasn't given us the final notice yet, for His mercies are new every morning, and He desires that all men be saved and come to the knowledge of the truth (I Timothy 2:4). Nevertheless, one day, for all of us, there will be a final notice, and we truly will have no more chances to take care of business. Fortunately, we have a God who continually serves us notice to take care of things while we have a chance. Unfortunately, none of us know when that final notice will come.

Finding the Wills of God

The title seems a misprint. Does God have more than one will? Yes! There at least 3 different ways to speak of the will of God...

1) There is a SOVEREIGN will of God. There is nothing that can keep His ultimate will from coming to pass; it is this will that is *going to happen no matter what*. He actively causes something to occur or He permits something to occur or He prevents something from occurring, and He is behind it all. This is the *hidden* will of God. God keeps His own counsel about some things, and no human being is privy to knowing God's mind here. In both Old and New Testaments writers ask, "Who can know the mind of the Lord?" (Job 38:4 and Romans 11:34, as examples) God *does* sometimes allow people to die in car wrecks, but He saved you. *Why?* We don't know. It's His sovereign choice. People get cancer. One lives and one dies, even though the saints prayed

for both. All we can say is that it was God's appointed time for one to leave this earth and it wasn't time for the other. We have no better answer than that. When will Jesus return? We know it is God's declared will, but it is His hidden will, because Jesus Himself makes it plain that no man knows the day or the hour of that return. Nobody knows when God will pull the trigger, and anyone who claims to know is someone to run from. The other thing about God's sovereign will that affects us tremendously today is the fate of the USA. We do not know if God will bring great revival to America, allow further persecution of His people, make America great again, or continue to allow America to self-destruct. It is wholly up to Him. Who wins the next election? Who will control the narrative? Will we descend further into anarchy? Only God knows. It happen according to His sovereign will.

2) But there is also the PRESCRIPTIVE will of God. This is the will of God that *He has made plain through the Law.* It is God's will that...
   a) We not steal, lie, or commit adultery—Exodus 20
   b) We obey our parents in the Lord—Ephesians 6:1-2
   c) We put Him first in all things and love Him supremely—Matthew 22:38
   d) We love our neighbors as ourselves and love our enemies—Mark 12:31
   e) We repent of evil and do good—Matthew 3:2
   f) We pray without ceasing, rejoice always, and give thanks in everything—I Thessalonians 5:16-18
   g) We serve others—Matthew 20:26
   h) We be hospitable and love without hypocrisy—Romans 12

Just as it is a fool's errand to ask God to reveal His sovereign will before events unfold, God does *not expect you to pray about these aspects of His will.* Someone attacks you, verbally or otherwise. There are times to defend yourself, but you do *not* need to ask if God wants you to forgive that person (He does). You are a child and your parents want you to take out the trash. Don't wait for some thunderbolt of revelation from the skies on whether you should do your chores (you should). You don't need to get special revelation about whether God wants you to cheat on your spelling test, or whether you should have sex outside of marriage, or whether you should go to church or tithe. God has *already* made all those things abundantly clear in His word. Don't pray about tithing. Tithe. Don't seek God's face about whether to be faithful in church attendance. Just come be faithful.

An important aspect of His prescriptive will is that *we can thwart it*. His laws are binding in that they are not going to change and as His children we should obey them, thus we have no authority to defy His will, but we do have the ability to defy His will. We know we are to be faithful in attendance, but we fall out of the habit. We know we are to tithe, but we keep back part of the tenth for ourselves. We know we are to accept others as Christ accepts us, but we decide to hold a grudge. We decide to cheat on taxes or tests, or business dealings. We never have the *right* to stand against the will of God, but we sometimes do so anyway. This is part of the answer to the enigma of God's will being that none should perish but all have eternal life, of God's expressed will that all come to repentance. It is His will, but will it always occur? The answer is no, because men have free will too. Sadly they choose to block this aspect of God's will.

3) The 3rd major type of will presented in Scripture is God's DISPOSITIONAL will; the will of God that comes from His *character and attitude*. This describes what *pleases* God. For example, God does not delight in the death of the wicked, even though He ordains the death of the wicked because He is a just God. He is pleased with our obedience, and displeased by our disobedience. This is the part of God's will mentioned in Romans 12:1-2. When we are transformed by the renewing of our minds we prove (or demonstrate or illustrate) the good,

acceptable, and perfect will of God. What does this look like? Well, you can actually follow God's prescriptive will without understanding or following His dispositional will. Let's illustrate it this way:

a) Can you give without being a cheerful giver? YES, but God delights in a cheerful giver. So you could follow the prescriptive will of God without following the dispositional will of God by giving cheerlessly.

b) Can you honor father and mother by taking out the trash, but do so with a grumpy, complaining attitude? YES, but God loves when we are zealous for good works and obey parents out of delight for God's word and respect for their authority.

c) Can you pray without ceasing without praying in the Spirit in faith; pray like the pagans, repeating a mantra supposing you will be heard for your many words? YES, but God obviously prefers that we pray in the Spirit and in faith.

d) Can you not steal, not lie, and not cheat in school and yet at the same time not do your work heartily as for the Lord? YES, but God wants you to learn to do it heartily unto Him. He does not want robots, but loving children who give everything they have to serve Him and honor Him.

Do you see the difference? It is God's express will that you not only serve but do so *gladly*. It is God's will that you give *cheerfully*. It is God's will that you walk with Him because you love Him and delight in Him rather than just out of a sense of duty. When you walk in this will of God, then you can answer questions like these more readily, questions not answered directly in His Word...

1) Do I attend this college or that one (or go work or go into the military or ___)?

2) Do I continue to date that girl or guy or move toward marriage with them?

3) Do I take this job or that one?
4) Is it time for me to move on to a different job, career, to retire, or do I stay put for awhile?

These and other questions are very important to us, and God cares about them because we do. So how do we know His will in these areas that are not specifically mentioned in the Bible? Here's my take…

First, ask God and He just might show you. That's a no-brainer. Many years ago I asked the Lord whether Gwynne was the one for me, and I believe He gave me the go ahead in our relationship to move toward marriage. That being said, an important question to answer is, "Does anything in this decision go against the expressed will of God in Scripture?" Well, it says don't get into deep relationships with unbelievers, but Gwynne was a dedicated Christian. I knew that God didn't want me to date or marry someone who wasn't totally sold out to God. Gwynne was certainly good on that point. God says in an abundance of counselors there is wisdom, so I asked mentors what they thought, and got the green light. My parents were very fond of her as well. Her dad gave the go-ahead (but told us to wait until she finished college, which we did). And now we've been married 41 years and have 11 children. I guess the recipe for finding God's will in marriage was a good one for me!

Submit to God's sovereign will. You can't change it anyway. Follow God's prescriptive will, gladly fulfill God's dispositional will, calm down, and God will lead you in the rest. Money, time, interests, talents (or lack of them), the counsel of intimates (especially if you're married—always consult your spouse), open and closed doors, all of these things and more can guide you. In the end, *you* must decide what is God's good, acceptable, and perfect will for you. Just keep renewing your mind and do what you know God wants you to do. The rest will work out, even though the path might seem meandering at times.

Holding Pattern

Recently at camp our speaker told an interesting story. He flies across the country a lot, and on this particular flight was especially anxious to make it to an intermediate destination so he could catch a connecting flight. He had put together a rather tight schedule, always a recipe for anxiety when depending on the vagaries of air travel.

So of course his plane, already a tad late, began to circle the airport instead of land. The pilot came on the intercom and told the passengers that they were in a holding pattern. This did not suit our speaker, who kept checking his watch and becoming more and more upset. "What will I do if I miss my next flight? I am the main speaker at the conference tonight and have to be there", he thought. "Lord, what are you trying to do to me? Can't You hurry this thing up?"

The minutes slowly ticked by, and the plane continued to circle. Finally the pilot came back on to assure the passengers that they would indeed land eventually, but that they were allowing a storm to pass underneath. There was simply too much turbulence for them to land safely at this time.

Unfortunately for our speaker this news was not what he had hoped for. Fortunately, he was a speaker, and speakers are always looking for good anecdotes and stories to tell to illustrate spiritual truths. This situation was a perfect illustration of a divine principle. We so often are blinded to reality because we do not have all the information we need to see it. As a passenger he was blissfully unaware of the storm and the turbulence that threatened them. Had he been the pilot, with superb skills and knowledge of the weather, he would have understood that being in a holding pattern was much preferred to spiraling out of control and crashing into the ground.

The pilot of that airplane had the passengers best in mind. His job was to deliver them safely to their destination and protect them from danger. We have a heavenly Pilot who has the same job description. We often get anxious and impatient when things don't go our way, and we can't stand the interruptions to our well-laid plans. But maybe we've built too tight a schedule together that doesn't take into account the delays inherent in our earthly travels, or perhaps we think our presence is too important, and that the event can't possibly go on without us. We must always remember that our Pilot knows more than we do, and that He at times puts us in a holding pattern for our own good. Silence from God is part of the journey with God. Being in a holding pattern doesn't mean the Pilot is against you. Silence may mean to buckle up and prepare for life's turbulence. In the silence God may be asking you to repent and reflect, as our speaker did when God spoke to him.

So let us relax a bit and enjoy the ride. There are no delays in God's schedule. The Pilot will see that we arrive at our ultimate destination on time, and wiser for the wait.

God's Most Amazing Attribute

God has many character qualities. What would you say is the most amazing of them all? It's not an easy question to answer, but I've picked one that strikes me as most remarkable. In Isaiah 6 the prophet sees God in the temple, and what is the first attribute of God that strikes him? That He is holy, holy, holy.

Holiness seems like such an other-worldly word, and fills us with awe and a type of dread in a way. It is a word at which we instinctively shy away. The Hebrew word is KADOSH, meaning "to be set apart for a special purpose."[108] Things in the Bible can be set apart for good or evil. In the judgment God sets apart those who know Him from those who do not know Him. The temple furniture and utensils were holy to the Lord, set apart for special use in worship. Israel was holy to the Lord, set aside to bring God's truth to nations. You and I, if we belong to Christ, are holy to the Lord, as I Pet 2:9 says, set apart to call forth the praises of the one true God.

To be holy is to be separate. And of all things that are separated, special, holy, God is the most holy. The Hebrew language doesn't use superlatives. It doesn't say this cake is good, but this cake is better, and then this last cake is the best. Instead it would say cake #1 is good, cake #2 is good good, & cake #3 is good good good. So in Isaiah 6:3 when the seraphim describe what God is like, they say He is holy, holy, holy. Other things or beings may be set apart, but God is **SET APART**!

We see this all through Scripture. God as Creator is holy, because only He can create a universe. God is holy as He deals with Adam's fall, because only He can correctly deal with sin. God is holy in accepting Abel's offering and rejecting Cain's, because only God can decide what a proper offering would be. This pattern runs all the way through the Bible, with God demonstrating His holiness during the Flood, the Passover, the parting of the Red Sea, the provision in the wilderness, the use of prophets, priests, and kings in the history of His people, the coming of Christ, the cross, the grave, and the empty tomb, and finally in the picture of heaven in Revelation, where the elders continually say holy, holy, holy is the Lord God Almighty, who was and is and is to come.

We can correctly label all other attributes of God as holy ones. He has a holy righteousness (He *always* does what is right); He demonstrates holy mercy (only He can truly pardon sin); He is holy in His faithfulness (we are sometimes faithful, He is always faithful to His promises); etc. And how grateful we should be that God is so different from us. If we were God we might show our wrath at the sin of man in a vindictive way, and immediately bring carnage on all men without being just. God has anger, but it is perfectly just, and in the great Judgment Day He will be perfectly just as He expresses it. And God has a holy love as well.

In our love we often *dote* on the object of our affection, whether a girlfriend, a spouse, or a child. We elevate the loved one so much that we are afraid to confront wrong behavior when necessary. But God's love is holy; therefore He is not afraid to discipline those He loves. Proverbs 12:6, "For whom the Lord loves He chastens, and scourges every son whom He receives." God is not afraid of our anger or our pouting. His love is holy, so He disciplines us for our good. Sometimes we love something or someone only for what we can get from it or them. It is a selfish love, sometimes a manipulative love. God in His holiness never loves that way. God's love is always for the good of the beloved, even if it costs Him. He's a God of holy love.

So praise Him for His holiness. Because He is holy all the rest of His attributes are perfectly balanced and higher and better than ours. We can trust God, and draw near to Him, because He is holy.

Lilies of the Field

What a wonderful May and early June we've just experienced. At our house we've had rain evenly dispersed without much hail, mixed with bright sunshine and relatively calm winds. It's been wonderful weather.

Oh how the weeds love it! Our community garden is covered up in them, and we find ourselves hoeing and pulling with a frenzy to expose the okra and squash and peas and remove their competition. It is a reminder of Jesus' Parable of the Sower, where the good seed grew up in some soil, but the weeds choked it out. (Matthew 13) Yes, weeds are a problem, and the rain makes them more of a problem than ever.

BUT...the rains also stimulate the growth of wildflowers. They are everywhere, and they bring joy and beauty to the landscape. The whites and yellows and blues and purples and reds are abundantly represented in the fields between here and Amarillo. We all know that it may not last too long, because the climate can get brutal in our long, hot, often dry summers.

So let us enjoy the beauty of the flowers while they are here. Jesus pointed out the lilies of the field as having more beauty than Solomon in all his glory. Even some weeds have lovely flowers. The Silverleaf Nightshade has attractive purple flowers, and the Prickly Poppy has charming white ones. Even thistles have flowers that some consider nice. None of these plants would be a favorite of gardeners, but their flowers still lend a graceful elegance to the land as we drive by. Flowers remind us of the results of rain—the beauty of the regeneration of living things.

The biologist would say that the flowers are a wonderful adaptation to achieve pollination and seed production. The poet would say that the flowers speak to us in a charming language that is all their own. But the Christian would say that the flowers, like all of nature, point us to the God who lavishes on us more beauty than the richest man who ever lived could demonstrate. Don't spend excessive time complaining about the weeds, but look to the Creator who makes the lilies...and brings the rain in its season so they can grow.

Beautiful bluebonnets

Right and Wrong

What is right? What is wrong? How do we know for sure how to tell the difference?
1) God's word is the TRUTH. ***John 17:17***
2) God LOVES righteousness. ***Psalm 11:7***
3) God's LAW is holy and good. ***Romans 7:12***
4) Is cheating wrong? ***Proverbs 11:1***

5) Is lying wrong? ***Exodus 20:6***
6) Is obedience to parents right? ***Exodus 20:12; Ephesians 6:1-3***
7) Is being kind to others right? ***Ephesians 4:32***
8) Is giving your tithe and offerings right? ***Leviticus 27:30***
9) Is standing up for God and His truth right? ***Ephesians 6:13***

And we could keep going with this list and write a whole book about what is right and wrong. But wait! There's already a book in print about that. America is in trouble because its citizens have followed their ancestors Adam and Eve in thinking they can come up with better definitions of right and wrong than God can. If God says it in His Word, we can bank on it. It will save us a lot of time in trying to define right and wrong ourselves.

The Will of God in Suffering

Suffering is not only allowed by God, in many cases it is His will. How can a compassionate God act in a way that causes pain? Some have said this is the hardest question of all to answer, but we have many insights:

Scripture doesn't always give the "micro" reason for a particular suffering. Why doesn't He heal *me*? Why didn't He intervene on *my* behalf? Why has *my* suffering lasted so long? *Why him and not me? Why now?* The great theological answer to all these perfectly reasonable questions is *we don't know*. But we do know *in general* why God allows suffering. He is NOT silent on this point at all.

1) **Suffering brings faithful believers into deeper understanding and relationship with Him** (Job). If the goal of life is to know the only true God and Jesus Christ whom He sent (John 17:3), then *if for no other reason* it's a good reason for God to allow suffering if it helps us know Him better. Just because we do not know the specific reason for a suffering does not mean a good reason doesn't exist.
2) **We know God wants us to become more like Christ.** We are predestined to be conformed to His image, so if Jesus was made our perfect high

priest by His continued obedience through suffering (Hebrews 5:8-9), shouldn't we expect to also suffer? We cry out for God to *deliver us*, when what He is seeking to do is *transform us*. He doesn't merely want to *move us* out of our suffering; He wants to *change us* through it. God is more concerned about your *holiness* than your *happiness*. His goal is your *eternal character*, not your *immediate comfort*.

3) **God wants us to fully rely on Him.** When we are prospering, healthy, and everything is going well, it is easy to think we don't need God. New cars, nice houses, and money in the bank feed this lie. It's when we suffer that we see our need for God. Suffering shows us we need God in a way that prosperity never could.

4) **God wants us to repent.** The first call of both John the Baptist and Christ was *repent*. You can't enter the kingdom unless you do. God permits suffering in the world to *warn the world* of the impending judgment. He uses it to call people to repentance. C. S. Lewis says, "We can ignore... pleasure. But pain insists upon being attended to. God whispers to us in our pleasures, speaks in our conscience, but shouts in our pain: it is His megaphone to rouse a deaf world."[109] Suffering is God's megaphone to get this world to wake up, listen, and repent.

5) **God wants us to see His glory on display.** The disciples meet a man born blind, so they ask whose fault it is. Jesus said it was no one's fault. The blindness was to demonstrate to others that He was the Light of the world (John 9). When Lazarus falls ill, Jesus doesn't come to his rescue. He allows Lazarus to suffer and die. But the suffering doesn't end there. Lazarus' family, including Mary and Martha, are heartbroken over their loss (John 11). So, why does Jesus orchestrate all of this suffering? He tells us, "It is for the glory of God, so that the Son of God may be glorified through it." (John 11:4)

6) **Being part of God's permissive will as the effect of sin.** Genesis 3 tells us suffering is the result of mankind's rebellion against God. Mankind (and that includes you and me) chose to reject God's commands, the world became corrupted by sin, and humans have suffered ever since. God's chosen people suffered when they

disobeyed the Law of Moses (Deuteronomy 28). We suffer too when we decide to borrow too much money or not save some back or engage in relationally stupid behaviors or when we go against sound counsel in pursuing a relationship that others see as bad for us. God specifically warns us about the wages of certain sins, but we sometimes ignore the warnings and therefore must pay the price. Sowing wild oats only yields wild oats, which aren't really great to eat. It is important to note as well that people sometimes suffer from the wrong choices of *other* human beings, even though God often uses the resulting suffering for good (Genesis 50:20). Joseph's brothers were cruel to him, Potiphar was unjust to him, and the butler forgot him, but Joseph felt in the end it all worked for good. Sometimes the outcome of growing up in an alcoholic home is ministry from those who have been through so much. They are able to help others in ways some cannot.

7) **Believers suffer because of the jealousy and hatred of certain people who reject the Christian faith** (Acts 7:54-60). It has been God's allowed will from the very beginning of Christianity for believers to be persecuted, in part as an evidence or testimony of faith to others (Hebrews 11). The early disciples believed it was an HONOR to suffer shame for His name. It is an honor, and an opportunity to put our money where our mouth is. Do we really believe or not? Suffering is a way of proving that we do, and what incredible testimonies have inspired and convicted others by the faithfulness of believers despite suffering.

8) **To prepare followers of Christ for the glory of Heaven** (2 Corinthians 4:17). Heaven is eternal. We want to be as prepared as possible to enter it. We want our character formed as fully as can happen on this side of eternity. Part of that forming process is suffering. Part of the reason we are ready for heaven is the serious pains in our own lives, serious difficulties that we have not been able to solve, serious sorrows. Sorrow does something to you if you learn from it; it tenderizes your heart, plows up the ground so it's

ready to receive the seed of God's Word, and that Word grows up and brings fruit.

9) Lastly, speaking of God's will in regard to suffering, **for believers to grow they must live in a world where suffering happens.** We cannot be generous unless there is someone who has less than we do. We cannot show compassion unless there is someone who needs caring for. The suffering of others often brings out the best in humans. How many great organizations that have done great work for humanity have sprung up from the heart of someone who noticed the suffering of a group of people and wanted to do all they could to alleviate it? This is actually part of our being made in God's sacred image. The bible in a nutshell is that "God so loved the world that He gave..." (John 3:16) God did not remain an aloof spectator of our suffering, but fully entered it, giving up His station, to experience all that we experience. When we, who are made in God's image, act out of His compassion, we imitate Him, and we glorify Him.

So why would God in His infinite wisdom not only allow suffering, but even be the causation of it at times? Well, we've seen lots of reasons. Think of them the next time you (or a friend) wonders what God is up to.

Telescopes

Psalm 34:3 encourages us to "magnify" the Lord and exalt His name together. We should never brag about what we or others can do, but let our boast be in the Lord alone. Of course we can't alter God; to magnify Him doesn't mean to make Him bigger or greater than He already is. To magnify Him means to make Him greater in our eyes, to make Him more prominent in our awareness. Magnification doesn't *make* objects bigger; it alters our perception of the object so that it *seems* bigger to us. When I say *"God, I magnify You"*, I am saying *"God, I am making You greater in my life, putting You first again, trusting in You to be bigger than my problems or anxieties."*

In Ezekiel chapters 37 and 38 the Lord magnifies Himself. Ezekiel 38:23 says "Thus will I magnify Myself, and sanctify Myself; and I will be known in the eyes of many nations..." God is referring to His unique ability to revive His people, put flesh on their "dry bones" described in chapter 37, return the people of God to their land of inheritance from the "four winds" or four corners of the earth, a prophecy fulfilled when the nation of Israel reconstituted after millennia of being scattered. In chapters 5, 12, and 17 Ezekiel had foretold this scattering, but he then tells of the God of mercy and power who alone can bring dead bones to life. Nothing is over until God says it's over.

And God does this to prove to the world that He alone is God. He is magnifying His name in the sense that He is showing the nations that nobody can resist His will. God doesn't need His ego stroked; that's not what magnifying is all about. But we need to magnify Him, especially this year where it has been so easy to magnify the cares of this world, our needs and the turmoil in our nation. It gets discouraging, defeating, and certainly distracting. When we magnify Him, we see Him as He truly is, and we remember how great and good He is, how He has the strength to provide for us in our weakness, how He can easily take care of our problems. The more we praise Him, the more we testify of Him to others so they can focus on Him too, the more we begin to see Him as big enough.

A microscope takes very small objects and magnifies them to look bigger so we can see them. This is not our job. We are not taking a very small god and trying to make him visible. Our job is to be telescopes. Their job is to take immense stars and begin to make them look as big as they already are. God is plenty big enough to take care of our needs as individuals, and indeed the needs of the whole country. Let's be telescopes and begin to see Him that way. And then show the world what a big God we serve.

The Lord's Offenses

Does the Lord say things to you that are amazing, that make you smile, that warm your heart, that make you realize how blessed and favored you are? Of course. He says you are children of God (John 1:12), that all things work together for good (Romans 8:28), that you were chosen (I Peter 2:9), created in His image (Genesis 1:27), and that you are His friends (John 15:15). BUT...Matthew 13:57 says the people were *offended* at Jesus because of some things He said.

Does the Lord say things to you that bring you up short, that humble you, that cause you to cringe, things you don't want to hear about yourself, things that offend you? He sure does.

My daughter Rachel and her husband Seth were talking about Matthew 13:57 not long ago and made a wonderful point: when we are offended we stop the blessing the Lord wants to bring. The people of Jesus' hometown were offended at Jesus because they thought they knew who He was. Some had grown up with Him. But He offended them when He announced He was Messiah, and made demands on their lives. Do we have the same problem? Are we so comfortable with the compassion of God that we forget He is also a God angry with the wicked every day? (Psalm 7:11) It says God judges the righteous as well. Part of His job description is to decide if a path we are taking is good or bad for us, and stop us from the wrong path, just as an earthly judge is responsible to bring the law against a lawbreaker so he will change his ways. If God's love was a soft love that never pushed back against our foolishness, how out-of-balance He would be! Proverbs 22:15 says a godly father drives the foolishness from the heart of a child who is bound up by it. Only an irresponsible father fails to discipline his child, and God is not irresponsible.

By its nature a rebuke is offensive. It brings us up short. While some of our grandkids were here we asked them to go upstairs to quietly read, since they were being too rowdy downstairs. Boy, did this bring back memories of days gone by! They all took books upstairs to read, and within minutes were racing up and down the hallway, out of control. Gwynne decided she'd had enough, and she went upstairs for some "training". What happened? The running and yelling stopped abruptly. The behavior changed radically. The children aligned themselves with the expectations and demands of the one in charge. They realized that G.G. was not going to put up with their nonsense. Perhaps they were offended that they couldn't run around like wild Indians anymore, but nevertheless, they did what they were supposed to do.

So rather than be offended by the hard sayings of the Lord, we should be guided and trained by them. Let it never be said of us that we were offended by what He said, or what He did to discipline us when we were out of control.

The Perfect Blend

We serve a God who is the perfect blend of justice and mercy. We know He is a God of law and order because "the Law of the Lord is perfect" (Psalm 19:7), that the law was given by God to help His people prosper (Deuteronomy 4:1-8), that the law is given in part to help us learn to rightly fear God (Proverbs 1:7). God gave civil laws to the Jews so they would have specific instructions on everything from murder to restitution after theft to dealing with animals getting out of enclosures to damage of another's property to what to eat to remain healthy. The laws were meant to help a society function in a stable, safe, and just manner. Then there were ceremonial laws involving the sacrifice of animals. These laws were given to help the world understand the full work of Messiah when He came. And finally He gave moral laws, based on His own holy nature. These then were holy, just, and unchanging, and they encompass regulations against lying, stealing, perverse sexual behavior, etc.

So God is a God of law. He makes the rules, and we are supposed to follow them. But what happens when we break the rules, as we inevitably do? That's where the second part of God's nature is demonstrated. He is a God of law, but He is also a God of mercy.

Hebrews 4:16 says God's very throne is one of mercy. Jesus' ministry was one that demonstrated mercy on many occasions, with women caught in sexual sin, with tax collectors who had overcharged their clients, with those who had been gluttons and winebibbers. Our salvation depends on His mercy, according to Ephesians 2:4-5. David demonstrated that we can call on God's mercy when we have sinned grievously (Psalm 51). Micah 7:18 says it is the character of God to show mercy, asking, "Who is a God like You, pardoning iniquity…?"

Thankfully we have a God who is the perfect blend of law and mercy, justice and grace, firmness and tenderness, unmovable yet compassionate. Psalm 18:30 has it right: "As for God, His way is perfect…"

What Only God Can Do

My backyard has never looked better. I've been active in hoeing, pulling, weed-eating, mowing, spraying, fertilizing, and watering, so I'll take credit for being diligent to do my part. But there are some things only God can do. You know and I know that here in the panhandle of Texas you can water until the lake is dry, and it will certainly help things along, but when God sends the rain the plants respond in spectacular manner. I've been mowing my lawn twice a week the past couple of weeks, but what a wonderful "problem" to have. At least it's growing. It doesn't take much walking down memory lane to think of times when rain was scarce and the grass wouldn't grow at all.

One of my favorite movies is "Chariots of Fire", and one of the memorable lines in the movie is a comment by Harold Abrams' coach. When asked whether he could make Harold an Olympic champion, the coach responded by saying, "Well, we have an old saying son, 'You can't put in what God's left out.'"[110] How true. Good coaching can take a poor athlete and make a good athlete, or it can take a good athlete and make an outstanding athlete, but no amount of coaching can take the Bad News

Bears and really win a championship in one season. That's just a storyline for a movie. There is only so much the coach—or the gardener—can do.

And so it is with our lives. We are responsible to diligently learn more, work hard, and do all we can to see our lives grow to fruitfulness for the Lord. Jesus said God is glorified if we bear much fruit and point people to Him. But in that same John 15 passage He made it clear that without Him we can do nothing. A branch produces fruit only when it is vitally attached to the vine. The fruit comes from God, and all the straining and striving we can bring to the table won't change that fact.

> *Lord, help us to do our part; and help us even more to trust in You to do what only You can do. Send us the spiritual rain, and help us grow into the people You want us to be.*

Chapter Ten—
Lighter Moments

I have a philosophical bent by nature, trying to learn a lesson in all circumstances, whether colossal or humdrum. Because my career paths led me into teaching and preaching, there is always something to learn and ponder...and share. Some events just strike you as humorous, but even in the funny things in life there is often a lesson. One extended piece in this chapter deals with funny things our children and grandchildren have said over the years, the Howard version of *Kids Say the Darndest Things*. I've included in this chapter as well a separate piece about Laura, my 7th child, the one with special needs. Her life has dramatically impacted our entire family, and you will enjoy getting to know her a bit better by reading what her siblings say about her. Hers is a special story, and I've included it here because she is an unwitting master at bringing lighter moments to all around her.

Does God Even Know?

One of my grandsons recently illustrated a common problem we have. We had a family Christmas gathering, and the evening went well, with funny songs, lots of laughter, and a reading of the Christmas story by some of the grandkids.

Well, one of the grandsons spoke to his mother on their way home, saying, "Mom, I prayed to God when I was outside." Expecting a sweet and thoughtful response, she asked, "Oh yeah, what did you pray for?"

His reply was typical of the honesty and insight sometimes inherent in a child's thinking: "I said, 'God, please tell me what I'm getting for Christmas. *If You don't know, I'll ask somebody else.*'"

We laugh at the childish way he interacted with the Lord, but don't we all approach God that way at times? We come to Him for answers, but deep down we're not sure He has them, or if He does, we're not sure He will reveal them to us. Certainly the ways of God are mysterious, and many of the answers we seek to profound questions are not easily attained. Proverbs 25:2 reminds us that it is the "glory of God to conceal a matter, but the glory of kings is to search out a matter."

Why does God conceal a matter? Well, there could be a number of reasons, and we won't always know those reasons. Just because we don't understand doesn't mean good reasons don't exist for Him to hide things. But part of the answer to God's concealments lies in the second half of the verse. When we have to work to find a solution to our problem it is a glory to us. The biblical concept of glory is to have "weight."[111] It is to carry importance. So in a sense this verse tells us that the more we have to dig to find answers to questions, the more that process builds character in us and the more excited we are when we find the answers that we know are from God. The answers gain more weight in our expectation and experience, and so does the wisdom of God gain more of our respect.

If you've ever wondered why certain things are the way they are, maybe you need to dig deeper. There are answers, but sometimes you have to keep searching until you find those answers. As a teacher I sometimes asked questions that required a bit of digging for a student to solve. Many students gave up trying to figure out the problem, but the diligent ones who really wanted to know found excitement in closing in on the solution and were well-pleased when they arrived at it. It was a "glorious" experience for them, and taught them that problem-solving in life is both satisfying and fulfilling.

Don't give up too fast on the Lord! He purposely hides some answers, because it is your glory to find them, like a child discovering

Chapter Ten—Lighter Moments

the hidden Easter egg or the adult finding the buried treasure. Wisdom is there, waiting to be discovered. She says, "I love those who love me, and those who seek me diligently will find me." (Proverbs 8:17) So go ahead and ask God about it. He has the answer, even though He may require you to do a little digging to find it.

Half My Brain

Rush Limbaugh became famous for several quips, including "With half my brain tied behind my back just to make it fair."[112] Well, I've recently been trying that half-brain thing, and it isn't working out too well for me. I went to the credit union to get a cashier's check and the clerk asked me for my account number, which is my social security number. I've given that number out many times in my life, but that moment it left me. As I reddened in the face and fumbled for my wallet to see if my card was there, I got more flustered and thought, "I'll bet she thinks I'm some sort of crook come to take this guy's money." Thankfully my old card was there, finally discovered, and I could give the lady the information. I left the place shaken. What is happening to my brain?

But I was far from done. Last week Gwynne, two of my children, and my mother-in-law were heading to Amarillo for a family event, and Gwynne wanted to stop by Dollar General in Clarendon to pick up some things. I left her, went and picked up my youngest son, finishing up at work, and headed down the road toward Amarillo. We were talking about his day when my mother-in-law suggested that we might want to go back and pick up Gwynne, still at the store. Wow, it is one thing to forget your kid, but your wife!? Talk about being out-of-it! And I had to be reminded by a woman almost 90-years-old! Well, at least Gwynne had more time to shop.

The final straw occurred a few days later. A friend called to ask for help because he was out bicycling in the country and felt like he was getting overheated. He wisely wanted to exercise caution. Could I come with my pickup and give him a ride back to town? Of course. I asked where he was, found out he was 5 ½ miles out at an intersection with which I was familiar. So I set out. Along the way I realized I had failed to bring my cell phone (how foolish), but thought, "Well, I know where he is." Except he wasn't there. I looked all around that intersection, and he was nowhere to be seen. So I thought maybe he was at another intersection three miles off, that maybe he was confused because the heat had addled his brain. Not there either. I decided to return to the house to get my cell phone and try to reconnect with him, all the while imagining him dying of heatstroke while I dawdled about the countryside with my half-brain. On the road back home I found him, standing in the middle of the road, smiling. "I suppose you've been here the whole time?" I asked. "Yep, you drove right by me. I thought for a minute you were just messing with me, but then you turned and drove off and I thought you were testing my faith." "Well," I countered, "if you hadn't been dressed in camouflage I would have seen you." (He was decked out in a bright red golf cap and flaming red golf shirt). Thankfully he was okay and we could laugh about it.

But working with only half of your brain isn't a laughing matter. I'm glad for the old truism that the Lord takes care of those eat up with the dumb. I resemble that statement more every day. My half-brain experiment has been a dismal failure. How did Rush do it all those years?

Is This Where We Were Trying to Go?

I had a wonderful time the other day with two of my adult daughters and some of their children. We went to one of my favorite places in the panhandle, Palo Duro Canyon. I grew up hiking in the canyon every year, sometimes multiple times a year. The canyon teaches you so many things. You learn to be wise, to hike when it isn't too hot. Some have even died hiking Palo Duro at the wrong time of day, dehydrated and over-heated . You learn to be tough. Hiking up and down those trails taxes you physically and mentally. You slip and fall sometimes, or scratch your hand on the rocks. You get halfway down a 2-mile trail and get tired, but there's only one thing to do, and that's keep going. You learn to enjoy nature. Deer, snakes, flowers, trees, bats, lizards—all these were part of our hike. We were eating after our hike and a roadrunner came by the table, chewing us out for being in his way. A while later he returned from the opposite direction with a grasshopper for his lunch. That's something you don't see every day at home. You learn to get dirty. Nature is not clean, but that's o.k. One grandson didn't like the dirt, but I told him if you grew up trying to stay too clean when you were young you might develop allergies as an adult. Something about the outdoors hardens you to the daily assault on your body.

And you learn the value of water. The canyon's river, sometimes dry, had a few inches of water in it this year and the grandkids loved playing in it, wading in it, trying to skim rocks on it. Under the bridge it was warm enough to enjoy dipping our feet in the cool liquid, but not so cool that we were uncomfortable. And it was there under the bridge, after over an hour of wading, throwing rocks, playing in the mud, laughing and having fun, that my four-year-old granddaughter, who had been having a blast, came up and asked me, "Pops, is this where we were *trying* to go?" It seemed as if she was disappointed.

Are we like that? Are we in a place in our lives that we enjoy, a place where we can be around family, laugh a bit, and kick our shoes off, only to get tired of the place and ask if this is all there is? Our party finally left the cool shade and the cool stream and hiked a trail with no shade and an increased temperature. My four-year-old didn't particularly like it. It was dusty and hot and seemingly never-ending to her. When we finished our hike and sat down to lunch I asked her if she liked playing in that stream more than she enjoyed hiking down that trail.

Be careful what you complain about. The Lord may have you in a great place. It may not be perfect in your eyes, but the alternatives could be much harder. Even a four-year-old can learn that lesson.

Where we were trying to go

Stinkin' Thinkin'

Ever clean out your refrigerator? I did that yesterday and found a few moldy things we had intended on eating as leftovers. Well, we left them over and over again, until they finally reached the statute of limitations. We know when even Max our dog won't eat it, it's past the point of redemption. I was sure glad to jettison some of those items. I'm sure you can relate.

How many of our thoughts or ideas need throwing away? Sometimes we have "leftovers" in our mind; items left over from our pre-Christian experience, items from the world that are no good for consuming any more. We need to do a good cleaning out and tossing of those thoughts, don't we? You know what I'm talking about…

"I can't…" God's word says "I can do all things through Christ who strengthens me." (Philippians 4:13)

"But…" God's word says "All the promises of God are YES in Christ"; there are no "buts" in God's promises. (II Corinthians 1:20)

"I am a failure." God's word says when a man falls down he has a companion to lift him up; so find that companion and accept his help to restore you to your task.(Ecclesiastes 4:10)

"There is no hope in this situation." God's word says it is Christ in you who is your hope of glory; therefore if you have Christ, you always have hope. (Colossians 1:27)

"I can't forgive them…" God's word says we are to forgive as Christ forgave us; to declare that you can't forgive is to forget the degree to which God has forgiven you. (Ephesians 4:32)

"This trial I'm going through is too overwhelming." God's word promises that no temptation will come to you but such as is common to man, and that with the temptation God will provide the strength to bear and overcome. (I Corinthians 10:13)

"I am discouraged". Maybe you are, and maybe it's a struggle, but God's word says over and over again to not be discouraged, but rather to be encouraged in God and trust in His ability rather than your own. (Joshua 1:6-9)

"My resources are not sufficient." Paul admitted that on his own he was insufficient. But he also said that his sufficiency was of God. And God shall supply "all your needs according to His riches in glory in Christ Jesus." (Philippians 4:19)

Throw out the leftovers that are rotting in your mind! They stink, and nobody can walk in victory with stinkin' thinkin' filling their minds.

The Struggle

It was all going to save so much money. He wanted to build a nice fence around his back yard, one with a good footer so the dog couldn't dig his way out. He had the skills and access to the equipment necessary, so this was one do-it-yourself project he could handle. He had built fences for others before, and knew what he was doing.

So he rented an auger for his skid loader, hooked it up, and began to dig out holes for the thirty pipes he would use. Sure would be easier than digging them by hand with his post-hole diggers. On the third hole his auger found something...the sewer line. A big oops, but nothing he couldn't handle. He had rented an excavator to dig a trench for pouring his footer; he would use that to expose his sewer line so he could repair it. The excavator did its job wonderfully, and along the way tore up his water line. Well, so much for a nice easy day on the job! Water was shooting everywhere, and now he had a sewer line *and* a water line to repair.

He wanted to cry, but grown men aren't supposed to be weenies, so he stiffened his lip and got to work fixing the damage. Finally done dealing with the unanticipated setbacks, he returned to his original job of digging out post holes. And—you guessed it—his auger hit the gas line. He couldn't believe it. What were the odds of wrecking the sewer line, water line, and gas line all on one project!

And it got worse. It wasn't too expensive to repair the sewer and water lines, just time-consuming. The gas line had to be repaired by a certified technician. Cost: $1300. So much for saving lots of the money by doing it himself!

Every guy that has ever worked much with his hands can relate. Our best laid plans often don't pan out quite like we thought they would. We have a vision in mind of how the project will proceed, and then life comes along and kicks us in the teeth. It's a struggle. But there are always silver linings. Even with the added cost and hassle, it's still going to be less expensive for our friend than paying someone else to build his fence. And think of all the things he learned along the struggling way: like where his sewer line, water line, and gas line were located. Hey, at least he hasn't messed up the phone line or electric lines...yet.

Unenforced

We've been gone on vacation for the past week or so, and had lots of fun on our big road trip. We traveled through ten states and drove over 2500 miles and saw many new sights. It was good to get away for awhile and enjoy the beautiful country. One thing I was a bit concerned about as we headed north and east was entering a part of the country where people were more likely to demand that everyone wear a mask when out in public. Where I live most folks gave up on the masks quite a while ago, and I wasn't looking forward to putting the face covering back on.

Turns out I had nothing to worry about. Although we saw many signs that declared "Masks Required", we were never asked even once to put them on. There is a principle that every parent, every teacher, every authority figure must always keep in mind: you can make all the rules you want, but only those that are enforced are followed.

We rode an 1880 train from Keystone, South Dakota, to Hill City, South Dakota. At the train depots on both ends of the trip it was posted several places in big print that masks and social distancing were required during boarding and transportation. The train personnel certainly followed the mandate, but not one passenger did. They had returned to pre-pandemic mode, standing close to one another in line, sitting close to one another on the train, enjoying their day, heedless of the posted rule. And not one person running the train said a thing. They had surveyed the crowd and decided that it was in their best interest to just let sleeping dogs lie, so to speak.

The same dynamic existed at Mt. Rushmore. Again, several signs clearly denoted that it was federal law for people on federal property to mask up and social distance when in a crowd. Those signs were apparently talking to the wind, because in the entire time at Rushmore I saw exactly two people with masks on. Not even the federal employees working at the federal facility that posted the federal mandates had on masks. Kind of made me wonder why in the world those signs were still posted. Maybe the only real rule there at Rushmore was that federal employees would be in trouble if they took down the signs, so they left them up.

But the signs were to no effect. There is an old adage that rules are made to be broken. Maybe that's true, but it's also true that the only rules that get followed are the ones that somebody takes the time and energy to enforce. Coaches, parents and teachers should keep that in mind.

Wrong Way Max

We love our dog Max. He's a dog with a questionable background, no purebred for sure. But like most dogs of mixed heritage, he's personable, unassuming, and loves being with members of the family. He's not a lap dog by any means, but if you sit down outside he'll try to become one immediately. He's also fairly bright, in the sense that if he ever gets out of the yard he doesn't go far and he comes back after a few minutes of freedom. He knows who brings home the bacon, and who feeds it to him.

But in one thing Max isn't the brightest bulb in the chandelier: he chases birds. I don't know if a great ancestor was a bird dog or what, but he has always been fascinated with these feathery creatures that flit above his head. If one lands in the yard and begins pecking around, he stalks it and explodes like a shooting star toward it. The bird, with the obvious advantage of flight, is almost never caught. Like the gambling addiction, however, once in a blue moon he catches one, and the bird is a goner. This keeps Max hoping and chasing all day long every day.

But there's more to the story than that. Underneath Max's feet, right there in the back yard, we have a problem with pocket gophers. These extraordinarily irritating pests dig up the back yard, create mounds of dirt, and sometimes eat the roots off my trees (they've killed several over the years). To my way of thinking, Max should quit looking up and start looking down. Those birds are so hard to grab 20 feet in the air, but here for the taking are animals that we really need to be rid of.

But Max is hard to convince. I've talked to him and talked to him, pointed out the gopher mounds, encouraged him to turn his attention to something that could really help the family, all to no avail. He insists on wasting his time and energy focusing his attention in the wrong direction. Sometimes it's easier to spend your time on things that don't matter, even though you somehow think you are accomplishing something important. Sadly, Max is not alone in his misguided philosophy. Many people are distracted from the real enemy, the enemy with which they should be engaged, and they chase things that they have no business chasing. Scripture warns us of this. It describes Satan as one who masquerades as an angel of light. (2 Corinthians 11:14) To masquerade is to pretend to be someone you are not, to wear a mask so your identity is hidden.

All of us need to deal with the gophers in our yard and ignore the birds that are doing no harm. Ask God to give you eyes to see the true problems that need addressing in your life, and to give you diligence to run them off your spiritual land. Don't be like Max and always be looking in the wrong direction.

Reflections From the Quiet Corner

Wrong-Way Max

The Crazy Things Kids Say

Any family with little children experiences funny moments that no movie script writer could make up. Three and four-year olds are best at these unscripted moments, but they can come about with any relatively young kids, and whether you have a huge household of them or not.

Rachel, only four the first time she saw *The Sound of Music*, was heard singing at the top of her lungs, "I am 16 going on 17, I know that I'm not Eve," sort of the evangelical version of the song. Kids are notorious for getting things mixed up when they are three or four-years-old as they try to figure out how life really works. Stephen at that age once remarked about an upcoming celebration, "Santa Claus is going to come and say 'Happy Birthday!'"

Chapter Ten—Lighter Moments

Sibling rivalry is a real deal, and despite parents' best efforts at promoting harmony it goes on. Fortunately they can make up. Samuel was four when he decided he didn't like Rachel and spat at her while they were brushing their teeth. Dad and Sam had a serious talk about whether he was really glad Rachel was his sister. He decided he was glad and told Dad he needed to go tell Rachel something (she had left the room). Here's what he said, "Rachel, God wants you to be glad I'm your sister!" Rachel was a bit puzzled, but not as puzzled as she was at the next line, "Daddy said that somebody gonna take you away and I be sad and say 'Where's my Rachel?', but don't worry; somebody gonna bring you back." Oh well, as long as they were now reconciled.

One thing about it, when you convince everybody that kids are a good thing, they respond with excitement when another one comes along. When Stephen was born Samuel was excited not only because he had another sibling, but a brother. He told everyone, "We have a baby. His name is Stephen Mark. When he dits big I'm gonna play ball with him." When told Stephen was a little boy just like him, Sam responded, "No, he's not a boy, he's a brother."

Samuel also got a bit mixed up on directions once. Dad and Sam were playing baseball in the hallway with his plastic bat and ball when Sam was three, and Dad was trying to tell him the proper way to hold the bat. Dad said, "No, Samuel, hold the bat back behind you." Sam responded by moving his entire body backwards until he ran into the closet door.

But as mixed-up as they can be, children are often profound. Bekah was trying to learn about the significance of Bible events. She was not even three when she saw a picture in Sunday School of Jesus that someone had ripped. "Look, Mom, somebody teared up Jesus." She thought for a moment and added "Probly da soldiers did it." Oh how much they already know at that age...and how much they have to learn.

When Rebekah was young, ages two to three, she had the cutest way of speaking. She said "I feezing" when she got out of the bathtub. When it was time for the family to watch something together on TV, she was excited to watch the "woobie". She really loved the water, so when it was time to get ready to go to the pool, she quickly dressed, except she called it a "babing soup" instead of bathing suit. Even to this day if I am taking grandkids to the pool, I will tell them to get on their babing soups in honor of Bekah.

Reading a book about chaotic times is tame compared to going through chaotic times, and a family often goes through chaotic times. At least our family experienced some real craziness. Trying to get everyone on the same page was not an easy task, almost ever, and we're sure that it showed in strained voices at times. During one such moment Rachel wryly announced, "I know a family that needs to have their devotions pretty soon!" We all laughed, but truer words were never spoken. Speaking of out-of-control attitudes, Laura once told me, "Dad, your wife has an attitude!" I, of course, being the wise, experienced husband that I was, did not agree with Laura, because my wife always has a good attitude. At least that's what I'm told.

All children have their fears. It's amazing how an 18-month old is often too young to realize the danger the family dog presents, but then six months later, when they are eye level with those canines belonging to the canine, they are terrified. That happened to several of our children, and now has happened to several grandchildren. We had a funny experience one time concerning childhood fears when traveling near Carlsbad Caverns, New Mexico. We had decided to visit the cave because several of the family members hadn't been there. We were discussing how much fun it would be to explore this unique underground national park, when Josiah, who was only four at the time, said he was fine with going down there as long as "Bad Carl" wasn't home. We all laughed at that one, but Ruth's biggest fear was more serious, and we are glad it didn't come true. When she was six she told Gwynne that she had been quite afraid that on her next birthday she was going to turn into a boy! Gwynne assured her that a lot of things could happen on her birthday, but that certainly wasn't going to be one of them.

Chapter Ten—Lighter Moments

We went through probably fifteen years or more of some child spilling their drink at suppertime. Stephen, at ten months, enjoyed simply turning the "sippy cup" over and dribbling the drink slowly onto the floor. He was doing a physics experiment we're sure, because science became a strong point for him (he is now a doctor). By the time he was eight he had science down. He and Ruth had gone to the doctor's office with Gwynne and while waiting for the doctor, were looking at anatomical charts. Ruth pointed to the lungs and said "There's the heart," but Stephen corrected her, "No, Ruthie, that's the soul."

Meal times were memorable for other reasons besides spilling drinks. Bekah had an imaginary friend named "Creddy" who got into numerous dramatic escapades, and for whom we had to pray repeatedly. Creddy got very sick one time and Bekah chimed in, "we haven't prayed for her yet," so the prayer request being brought to the group, we stopped eating long enough to say a prayer, and with that Creddy recovered and we could resume our repast. Stephen's imaginary friend Johnny died nearly every night in outlandish fashion, including once getting eaten by a shark (we live 500 miles from the nearest ocean). Trying to empathize with Stephen, we would always look sad and give our regards to him and tell him how sorry we were about the loss of his friend. His unerring response was "It's okay, he's alive again." Sadly, Stephen resurrected Johnny only so he could invent a new way for him to die the next day. Stephen once told us Johnny couldn't go camping because he was sick. When asked what made him sick, Stephen said "'Cause he ate whales and sharks and camping is where the sharks are!" (We never quite figured out where the obsession with sharks came from).

Neither Bekah nor Stephen however could quite do the storytelling that Deborah did. She didn't just have an imaginary friend; she had an imaginary family. She often would talk about her "other dad, the one who was in jail." I hoped she wouldn't mention this in the grocery store to some stranger, or to my friends at church. I could hear the questions from them coming, "Bruce, are there things about you and Gwynne and the family you haven't shared with us?"

I had promised Samuel and Stephen that I would give them a "buzz" haircut when Samuel was six and Stephen three. Well, the clippers were old and kept pulling out Sam's hair, which obviously hurt, so I fiddled a bit with the system and gave a good push, only to discover that the clippers worked too well at that particular moment, and it was a very close buzz indeed. Since all the hair should be the same length, both Sam and Stephen got the shave of their little lives. Stephen looked in the mirror and kept falling down yelling "I'm bald, I'm bald!" In all the rest of their time at our home neither ever asked me for another buzz cut, or any other kind of cut for that matter.

Rachel was always a talker and good with vocabulary, especially since I taught biology and thought it fitting to teach her the names of her bones. One day at age four she said to Gwynne, "Mommy, we need to put a Band-aid on my knee. The Band-aid is going to peel the hurt off and God is going to put my knee back on. That is my patella." I haven't done an extensive study of this, but I'm assuming most four-year-olds don't know that the patella is the name for the knee cap. Rachel also had done some speculating as only a four-year-old can. Riding home one day she said, "Mommy, cars can't talk. Did you notice the reason? (Sadly, Mommy had not noticed) The reason is because they don't have a mouth. That's the reason." Makes sense to me.

Samuel also had a creative bent. He once told Gwynne he could smell Grandmother cooking, even though she was over 500 miles away. When asked how such a feat was possible, Samuel said "I can smell her cause I have an imagination!" But later he said he didn't have it any more because someone took it. Peter, age four at the time, also had an imagination, and one day was listening to Ruth and Gwynne talk about a canker sore in Ruth's mouth. Peter piped up, "Ruth Anne, you've got a kangeroo sore!"

It's funny how early in life people begin to think of marriage. In my experience usually it's the girls who fantasize about the event, but sometimes guys will engage. Stephen, aged three, decided he wanted to marry his sister Bekah, aged four and a half. Her response was, "I can't marry you. I'm going to marry Jesus." Hannah at three was just sure she was going to marry another three-year-old named Clay, who was not part of our family and for whom Gwynne provided child-care one year while his mother worked. Hannah would dress up in a miniature wedding gown and gather flowers for the event. Clay showed absolutely no interest in the upcoming nuptials, however.

This dreaming about marriage wasn't just something our children did; now the grandkids are involved. Sarah, Ruth's oldest, now age six, wanted to look at Ruth's wedding dress recently and talk about when she got married. "We need to go ahead and start planning now because it will happen before we know it." There is a lot of truth in that statement.

The influence of parental philosophies is strong. Not only attitudes about marriage are absorbed through osmosis by young children. When Stephen, our fourth, was born, we were officially in crazy land for having so many kids (little did we realize what was coming!), but we were sure glad he was here, and so was Rachel (a bit older than five when he arrived). Her response to his birth was "I just can't stay away from this baby. I just can't keep from looking at him because he is so precious. I just love him so much!" Out of the mouth of "babes" came some strong words of receiving another babe. Rebekah, about five at the time Peter was born, said that "When the baby has distractions (contractions), then I'll hold him real tight until he feels better." Bekah was also old enough to have heard some things about our country that weren't good. She was holding Peter and said "Mommy, I'm sure glad you didn't have a divortion" (abortion).

A few weeks later Bekah was giving Stephen lessons on how to hold young Peter. "Stephen, you don't hold the baby by the head! That's the way Indians hold babies because they don't like babies. You hold them like this."(Demonstrates) "This baby is an orphan and this is the way you're supposed to hold orphans." We were a little concerned about this "Indian" thing she had espoused. We certainly don't consider ourselves xenophobic. So Gwynne asked her "Where did you learn about Indians holding their babies by the head?" Bekah's response was, "Nowhere, I just taught it to myself." Gwynne said, "Oh, I see. Well, just don't let any Indians hear you say they don't like babies." Bekah, rather startled, responded, "They can't hear me, they don't live around here anymore."

Of course with babies always on the way for the Howard clan, the children pick up on women being pregnant. When Gwynne was pregnant with Rebekah, Rachel proudly announced to people in our church that there were babies in her tummy too (foreshadowing; she now has eight of her own). "I have five babies in my tummy, and they are going to come out pretty soon and then we will find out what their names are." As Gwynne and four-year-old Rachel were walking to the car she added "That was fun talking to the ladies about the babies in our tummies. I glad we have babies in our tummies. Daddy doesn't have babies in his tummy, but we do because we are ladies."

When Hannah was three, she told Gwynne one night that the older kids were eating too much, and that "They are going to get fat and have babies!" Gwynne informed her that was silly, boys couldn't have babies. Hannah responded with "Well, the ladies are." Now fast forward and listen to adult Rachel's resident philosopher, three-year-old Hope. Hope put a piece of fruit in her cheek last year and said, "Look, Mom, I've got a pregnant!"

Hannah, three, was watching Gwynne tear fabric into strips (Gwynne was making a crocheted "rag rug.") Hannah asked her what she was doing, and Gwynne said "I ripped it to shreds!" Gwynne repeated it a couple of times so Hannah would understand, but apparently that failed. Hannah said "I don't *want* to lick the bed." Just a wee bit of misunderstanding.

Hannah also had a bit of trouble concerning abstract ideas. She came in from jumping on the trampoline when she was three and said "Someone hurt my feelings." Rachel asked her where her feelings were. Hannah looked startled and said, "They're gone! Someone took them!" After being pressed on it, Hannah said "Lydia took them!" And then we discovered that Lydia had taken them to the church where they had been clothed and taken care of.

Chapter Ten—Lighter Moments

At the same age, Hannah was home when Rachel called from Texas Tech, where she attended college. Hannah was sad she didn't get to talk to her. But then Rachel called again and Gwynne told Hannah to get on the phone upstairs. Hannah was surprised to hear Gwynne (on the phone downstairs) on the phone too, so she asked Gwynne what she was doing. Gwynne told her she was on the phone. Hannah, thinking of her mother sitting atop of the phone, said "Mom, you're so…so…CUTE!" Hannah also wanted to go see the propane man when he came to fill the tank. Gwynne told Hannah to stay inside while she went outside to pay the man. When Gwynne returned Hannah asked "Did you paint the man?" Hannah wasn't the only one of our children who struggled to understand abstract ideas. Lydia helped me plant some flowers one spring when she was four. She had a delightful time helping Dad outside in the beautiful weather. Our big surprise came later when Gwynne was sharing Proverbs with Lydia and trying to explain how important wisdom is. Wisdom is a bit of a nebulous concept for a four-year-old, so Gwynne said, "Lydia, wisdom means you learn to plan ahead." Lydia looked very puzzled, remembering her gardening experience, and then smiled, "Mom, you're teasing me. You can't take someone's head and plant it." And it's absolutely true that we are not going to plant anyone's head anytime soon around the Howard house.

And then there was the time Hannah, Deborah, and Lydia dressed up to play Sleeping Beauty. Hannah, only three, wasn't old enough to play the lead role, but Deborah told her she could be Queen of the Fairies instead. A church friend dropped by the house about this time and asked Hannah what they were playing. "Dairy Queen", she said proudly.

These funny family events now occur with regularity in the lives of our adult children and our grandchildren. A couple of months ago Rachel's daughter Hope (three and a half) told Rachel from an adjoining room, "Mom, JoJo (age two) can't find her apple." Rachel countered, "Well, maybe you could help her find it," to which Hope retorted, "I can't. I took it from her." The philosophical turn runs deep in Rachel's kids.

When Josh was about five he asked Rachel, "Mom, why do flies always stare at us?" Rachel responded, "Um...I guess they are watching to see what you'll do...?" Joshua thought for a moment then said, "Oh, like, if you'll start dancing?" Maybe that's it. Now we know why flies stare.

I'm sure Josh learned to philosophize from Caleb, Rachel's oldest. When Caleb was seven and Josh five Rachel walked past their room and saw Caleb bent over tying Josh's shoes. Both boys were wearing caps turned around backwards, along with sunglasses. Rachel was informed by Caleb that they were trying to look better so Josh could get more girlfriends, "cuz he only gots five." Hope Josh doesn't get too popular. What would you do with more than five girlfriends (besides get in a lot of trouble)?

And then there was the time Seth discovered that Caleb and Josh hadn't cleaned up their room as he had instructed them to do. "Why did you two not do what I said?" Caleb responded, "Well, I'm very tired. I haven't slept since I turned six." Seth couldn't quite believe that, so he added, "Why do I have to come in here every morning then and get you up for school?" Caleb's answer? "Well, I've just been faking."

Rachel's third born, Andrew, learned a lot listening to Caleb and Josh. He and Gracie (Rachel's fourth) were sitting on the sofa when he was only about three, and he had discovered Rachel's i-Phone and was beginning to play with it, a taboo Rachel had made abundantly clear. Rachel came in and discovered the little miscreant, but Andrew alertly responded by saying, "Look, Mommy, someone gave you a present." Smart boy; or maybe he's just a smart aleck. Because there was the time Seth, Rachel's pastor husband, drove by a very large church in Amarillo with Andrew, who at the time was 10-years-old. Seth asked, "Andrew what would you think if you heard me preach in a big old church like that one?" Andrew's response? "The same thing I always think when you preach: nothing". Just a reminder that a pastor has to have thick skin and preach for the Lord, not for men (or their sons).

Mothers who are music leaders must also do their service unto the Lord and not for people. Rachel leads her church in singing praises during the services. When Josh was little, he said one day that he had been "speaking to Zach and some of the other people of the church" and that she was being "fired from music." Rachel asked why and he said she had been playing too many "sad" songs and it was making the older people nervous. We're happy to announce Rachel stayed in her job leading the praise and has cut down on the sad songs enough so that the older people are no longer nervous in church.

Ruth told of her oldest, Sarah, trying to put her second youngest brother's tennis shoes on his feet so he could go play in the snow. He was giving her trouble, when she said in exasperation, "Obadiah, I'm trying to help you. Do not make this difficult." The two and a half-year-old didn't bat an eye when he retorted, "But I *want* to make it difficult!" Fair enough. Like I said, sibling rivalry is here to stay; and as Art Linkletter used to say, "Kids say the darndest things!" And sometimes they want to make life difficult for sisters…and parents.

Samuel and family

Stephen, Peter, Hannah's husband Chesson, and Josiah

Rachel, Ruth, and Bekah

Chapter Ten—Lighter Moments

The World According to Laura

We didn't know it at the time, but Peter, child #6, was the half-way point in our child-bearing. Peter had some physical problems with seizure activity during his early months, and it was a traumatic time for us all as we watched helplessly, prayed, and finally the Lord and the doctors were able to get things under control. It certainly wasn't a time to be thinking about another baby, but, since the Lord absolutely has a sense of humor, Gwynne got pregnant again right on schedule. Her pregnancy with baby #7 was different. The second half of our child-bearing would be different too; special. And our family would never be quite the same again.

Baby #7 was head-up in the womb and not head-down, and the baby simply would not "engage" in the last weeks of the pregnancy (for the baby to engage is for it to turn upside down and prepare to be born). The midwife suggested playing music down near the birth canal, because sometimes babies turn to listen to the music (how's that for a crazy thing?). Doctors tried to physically turn the baby (Gwynne certainly did *not* enjoy *those* doctor visits!). We prayed, we hoped, but all to no avail. The baby stubbornly refused to turn (oh, the foreshadowing!). How much we would discover about the stubbornness of baby #7!

Well, since the baby was breach, doctors said we'd have to have a Caesarean birth, something we had not experienced, and something we did not particularly look forward to. September third finally came around, the date for the surgery. I had been there for all the other births, and Gwynne wanted me there for this one, so I dutifully held Gwynne's hand while they opened her up, and I actually managed not to pass out during the process. Laura Elizabeth was born, cried her first cry, and entered the world. Everything was fine; baby and mother doing well, so after a time I went home to tend to the rest of the brood.

Preparing to return to the hospital the next morning, I talked to Gwynne on the phone and first heard the words "Down syndrome." Is anyone ever really ready to hear when their child is born that all is not going to be "normal?" Well, it was a body blow for sure. I got in the car and drove to the hospital with the rain coming down, and had an opportunity to vent a bit to the Lord. "God, thanks a lot! We've gone on this journey of faith; had this large family; nobody understands us, and now we've got a special needs child. What are You thinking?" I had experienced a few times in my life where a message from the Lord was very clear; not audible, but so clear there was no doubt about the origin of the communication. These had always occurred during times of crisis in my faith. I had heard clearly about dating Gwynne, heard clearly that she was the one God had for me, and heard clearly that we were to receive all the children He sent to us. I now heard again. "You have prayed since before your first child came along that your children would glorify Me. You do not know what it will take to accomplish that; but I do, and Laura will be a big part of it."

Well, needless to say, that was a calming voice when one was needed. From that time on I entered the unknown world of parenting a special needs child with resolve. What would she be able to learn? What special accommodations would be necessary? Would she need therapy, where would we find someone to work with her, and how would we afford it with so many other mouths to feed? What about her schooling? How could we give her the love and direction she needed? There were a thousand questions, and we had none of the answers.

But answers came, slowly and surely. After rounds of physical therapy, and speech therapy, and with the motivational help of her two nearest younger siblings Lydia and Deborah, Laura developed. It took her longer to walk than normal, longer to talk than normal, longer to do almost everything kids do who are normal. But she wasn't normal, so it was okay. She developed at her own pace, that pace accelerated by watching and copying Lydia and Deborah. You could see the wheels turning in her head. *"I'm older than they are, but they can already walk/talk/do more than I can. I'd better learn to do that too."*

Laura had great teachers at school, and she learned to read, learned to do basic math, and learned about relating to people in a work environment. She proved to have a bright and engaging personality that everyone enjoyed, and like all of our children, school was in her opinion the best of places to be. During Laura's senior year of high school there was an opening-day assembly in the auditorium for all kids and staff. Everyone was excited about the new school year, chatting with one another. I noticed Laura, sitting with her friends near the back of the auditorium, so I went to sit by her. She was talking incessantly about something as usual, and then read aloud from a handout everyone had been given. One of our basketball coaches was sitting behind her, (Coach and I had been conversing about the upcoming season for Lydia and Deborah) when the coach remarked "Wow, she reads really well." My reply was "Sure does, and you should see her spell! She probably can out-spell nearly every student in this room."

We often pay lip service to the expectations we have of "anyone." We say anyone can be president; anyone can accomplish anything; anyone can become… But it is often lip service only. When someone overcomes a handicap to accomplish something that for them is an amazing feat, we are often surprised. *"I didn't really think they could do that!"* Laura is an example of what can be accomplished in a special needs life when surrounded by "normal" children who were bright, energetic, and talented. Laura watched her siblings and simply carried on as she had seen them do. She walked later than they did, struggled to talk early and plainly like they did, and had to surmount obstacles they didn't have to face; but she persevered, *stubbornly* refused to be left behind, and in her own way found success.

I have wondered, with all the intelligent children we have, if Laura isn't the brightest of them all in a way. Had she not had Down syndrome she might have shown up everyone else. In a way, she does. She just uses her intellect in different ways. For example, don't tell her your birthday or anniversary if you don't want her to know it, for she has an amazing memory for them. I have trouble remembering the grandchildren's birthdays, but not Laura! Her memory for those things is well nigh photographic. And our church on Sunday evenings opens the service with fifteen minutes of "hymn favorites", where folks can ask to sing any hymn in the book. If you want yours sung first, you'd better be ready with the number, because Laura sure is. She has memorized virtually every hymn by number in the book, especially if we sing them somewhat often. "Laura, what's hymn #450?" "*I Need Thee Every Hour.*" "What about 340?" "*He Hideth My Soul.*" "644?" "*Count Your Blessings.*" It's very hard to stump her. Nobody else in our church can do that. I call it the blessing of the uncluttered mind. Laura doesn't have to worry about many of the things "normal" people do, so she turns her attention to other things. To say she is high functioning is an understatement.

And the impact she has had on her siblings! God always speaks truth, and when He said that Laura would have an extremely positive impact on her siblings He wasn't kidding. We have noticed that they are so much more sensitive to the needs of others than many of their peers. Bekah said she was not afraid of anyone different and that she learned not to be ashamed of anyone in her family. She probably wouldn't have had that attitude without Laura's influence. She, like other siblings, felt the need to protect Laura and stand up for her. She was always surprised with the amazing things Laura could do. It's easy to put people in the box and not let them get out, but Laura broke out of the box time and time again. Our other children learned not to assume what Laura could or could not do, because she did so many things we weren't sure she could do.

of course all Laura's brothers and sisters have a special place in their hearts for those who have special problems. Their career choices have demonstrated their wish to serve others. Their majors in college included teaching (one in Special Ed), medicine, psychology, and accounting, all service careers. Laura's oldest brother Samuel serves his country in the Army Reserve and is planning on getting his nursing degree. Serving others runs deep in the psyche of our children, and at least part of that desire to serve is from growing up around Laura.

Rachel, the eldest, pondered all the things she had learned watching Laura. One of the blogs in the chapter about family shares what she learned. Both Bekah and Stephen enjoy Laura's refreshing transparency and lack of guile, like Rachel and the rest of her siblings and anyone else who knows her well. She is genuinely compassionate and loving, and always herself. Her innocence in conversation and manner are disarming. Stephen said "There is a degree of comfort and ease that she brings to a conversation, and you can see people visibly relax when they realize this about her. It makes her fun to be around and talk to." Laura has an adult friend who loves to talk to her because she says it helps in some crazy way to calm her and ease some of the pain she had experienced in life.

Ruth is the sibling with the Special Ed degree, and she adds concerning Laura, "I think the greatest blessing and lesson I've learned from Laura is how to love the Lord in a childlike way. She reminds me of Psalm 24:3-4,'Who shall ascend the hill of the Lord? Who may stand in His holy place? The one who has clean hands and a pure heart, who does not trust in an idol, or swear by a false god. They will receive blessing from the Lord...' She convicts me by the innocent way she admires and loves the Lord and makes me want to do the same." Ruth definitely credits Laura with much of the motivation she had to get a degree helping children who have special needs.

Lydia, who is 19 months younger than Laura, has a unique view of her..."In my time as a teacher, I have worked with many students with special needs. People often comment in surprise on how "good" I am with them, even when the relationship is just starting out. At first, I was confused by this. I didn't feel like I was doing anything special or different from another educator. Yet as I began to observe more closely, I saw how others often looked at these students. It wasn't that they were mean or rude necessarily, but many just didn't seem to see them, or they seemed to be too uncomfortable to interact with them. Even administrators would come into the classroom acting solemn, rarely smiling and saying little before leaving again. As a general rule, people just don't seem to know what to do with special needs folk, so they do little to nothing. Another trend I noticed was that for every person I talked to who worked with special needs students on a regular basis, they had a family member or someone very close who also had special needs. It made me realize one of the many things Laura has done for me. She bridges the gap to strangers with special needs. Instead of seeing them as some avoidable 'other', or people who aren't people, I see her in them, and I see their humanity. Even before I meet them, I see them as people with souls and personalities and likes and dislikes. This makes the relationship much easier to form. I am not put off or intimidated. Rather than feeling discomfort, I immediately feel a connection to anyone who bears the mark Laura does. And regardless of what I don't know, I do know that they are precious and valuable. Laura did that for me. I like to think that being a Christian is enough, or that I would be a 'good person' regardless, but knowing Laura, loving Laura, gives me a head start when it comes to loving others."

When Lydia was in college she wrote about a particular incident involving Laura when they were both young that gives insight into her appreciation of her special sister...

"I walked beside Laura as we made our way through the buzzing cafeteria, breakfast trays in hand. At school, I stuck as close to her as I could. The kindergarteners and second graders usually had their own schedules, but thankfully meals and recess overlapped, so at least then I could protect her.

We chose a table and sat down beside two first grade boys. I knew Freddy (not his real name) because his sister was in Laura's class, and they were friends. She was nice to Laura, and I thought he might be too, but I was wrong.

As we took our seats, Freddy scowled. "We don't want her to sit with us," he said, looking at my sister. My face went red and I clutched my tray tightly. My knuckles turned white. "Come on, Laura. We don't want to sit by these idiots anyway," I said.

I spit the words out, hoping they would sting as much as his had. Hot tears slipped out as we found another table. Laura's face was downcast, but she said nothing. I wasn't sure if she had understood. "I love you, Laura. You're my best big sister." She smiled and bit off a piece of pancake stick dipped in syrup. She was happy again.

I wasn't hungry anymore, but I absent-mindedly chewed and swallowed as we sat in silence. Ever since I had started school, I had struggled with how people treated Laura. At home, we all understood that she had Down syndrome, and that meant she was special and sometimes she didn't understand. I had to explain it to Deborah because she used to get mad at Laura for not understanding or for getting out of trouble when she did something she shouldn't have. I had to explain to her that it's because Laura's brain doesn't work like ours. Some things are harder for her.

But not everything. Some things were easier for Laura because of her disability. She was only eight years old, but she knew all nine of my siblings' birthdays, and she knew more phone numbers by heart than Mom or Dad. We were all proud of Laura, and we didn't mind about her being special.

But school was different. People didn't care how good Laura was at remembering birthdays or phone numbers. They just cared about her being different, and they didn't really like it. Her second grade friends thought it was funny. They liked to ask her to say words that she couldn't so it sounded like ones she shouldn't say. I didn't think that was one bit funny. Laura didn't think it was funny either, she just didn't have the words to say so. But I know she didn't. She knew when people were laughing to be mean and when they were laughing to be nice. I could tell because sometimes she smiled and laughed right along with them and sometimes she didn't.

I never laughed with those second grade girls. They were mean to Laura, and it made me mad. That's why I was glad that we had lunch and recess together. I could play with Laura and keep her away from her 'friends', as she called them. That's another thing that Laura is better at than other people, being a friend. She never holds a grudge or gets mad (well, not normally) or says mean things to hurt your feelings. She is everybody's friend, even the mean second grade girls. I wish she wasn't, though. Then it would be easier to protect her.

I didn't have to protect her at church. Everyone knew Laura, but they didn't mind her being special. They loved her and knew how unique she was. And they knew that she was really good at making friends, so they liked that. I liked being at church when it was safe to play with my friends instead of watch Laura. I knew she was okay without me there.

Sometimes I wondered what it would be like if she didn't have her Down syndrome. I wondered if she would do my hair and teach me how to tie my shoes like I taught Deborah. Or maybe she would tell me her secrets, and I could keep them safe for her. Sometimes I secretly wished that Laura was normal so we could play together like other sisters did, without all the protecting from mean people who didn't like her disability.

I wished Laura could understand when she was doing something that people were going to laugh at or that she knew the things you aren't supposed to say if you want people to like you. But then I remember how when I first started kindergarten, a first grader was picking on me and Laura told them, "S-ss-stop being mean to my sister!" and I stopped wishing she was different.

Instead, I wish other people were different. I wish they didn't see only her disability instead of Laura. I wish they could laugh at all the funny things she says like, 'I walk backwards when I get nervous.' I wish they could just smile and be nice instead of say they don't want her to sit by them. If people were different, then no one would mind that Laura is, too.

We finished our food just as the first bell rang. "Goodbye, Lydia. I love you." Laura wrapped her arms around me, and I squeezed her tight. "Goodbye, Laura. I love you, too. I'll see you at lunch!"

I watched her until she found Mrs. Lollar and then I took our trays to the trash. As I walked out of the cafeteria towards the kindergarten classroom, I went by Freddy and made sure he saw me stick out my tongue."

Deborah, a little over three years younger than Laura, also has a special appreciation for her...

"Growing up with Laura has been eye-opening to say the least. Of course I remember times when I was so frustrated with her I wanted to pull her hair out (I think I tried once), but in retrospect her presence in my life has been one of the most precious gifts God has given me. First, Laura has taught me what it means to be authentic. Laura cannot walk into a room and be someone she is not. She may act like a diva sometimes, but she truly has no guile and it shows when she introduces herself unashamedly to everyone that crosses her path, whether it's the cashier at the store or the speaker of an event; when she tap dances in a room full of people without music; or when she fake cries in front of her family to get attention. She will walk up to a complete stranger and say, "Hi my name is Laura Howard. I am ____ years old." She is herself everyday – the good, bad, ugly – she doesn't hide it. She doesn't see people through the same filter most of us do, and I love it. It's refreshing.

She also has her own way of sharing her thoughts and feelings. Sometimes the message gets lost in translation, but one of my favorites that she often says is, 'I love your smile.' And she means it. I learned about God's love and patience while growing up with Laura. Like I said before, there have been times we've all wanted to rip her hair out in frustration (more so when we were younger and less mature) and in many ways Laura was and still is difficult to understand. Growing up, she was not always easy to talk to or negotiate with. I remember it being difficult to teach her boundaries and discipline. Yet God saw fit to give us daily practice in patience development. As I've gotten older, I've realized there are many people in life who are difficult to understand or get along with, and our human nature is to avoid them. God humbly shows us his great love for every person He creates by teaching us we all are recipients of His patience.

Our love for Laura (and anyone who is difficult to understand) is tested during those times of frustration. By God's grace, we've learned to see the things that make Laura who she is and love her for them instead of resenting her for things she cannot change. It is a treasure to see life through her eyes. When she writes people notes or letters she often says, "You are a gift to me, and that is God's gift to you." I don't fully understand it, but I absolutely love that she writes that way. It's from her heart and represents the unique qualities that God gave her to help us understand Him better."

Hannah, our youngest daughter, echoes that sentiment. "Disabilities are always viewed in a negative light. They are impairments, handicaps, abnormalities, and incapacities. However, Romans 8:28 says "We know that all things work together for good..." God can use our imperfections, whether physical, mental, or spiritual, to display His power and goodness. Although there were many difficulties that accompanied having an older sister with Down syndrome, if anyone is proof of God's love and goodness, it's Laura Elizabeth Howard. Anyone who knows her falls in love with her fun, kind personality. As a more timid and quiet person, I have always looked up to her for the ease and confidence she has even with complete strangers. Of course, there have been moments where that easiness with people who might be unknown assailants has been terrifying and one would wish Laura had a little more caution.

Another trait I admire about her is that she is always herself. While most people only show you a piece of themselves and sometimes an altogether lie, Laura is the most genuine person you'll meet. She doesn't put on a front to impress or manipulate, and she won't say one thing to your face and another behind your back. While she might not tell you that she ate your snack or took your shirt from the dryer, you can always rely on her bluntness when it comes to your acne or body odor. But aside from all these fun and exasperating traits, she is first and foremost, a Christian. Even when she has a hard time grasping reality or communicating her thoughts, she is deeply in love with the Lord. She has a heart for God and for people that is precious. She may not understand that our family is not Italian, but she knows who her Savior is, and she is a dedicated servant to the Most High. Her simple yet profound faith is stirring, and if I can be anything when I grow up, I want to be more like Laura."

Of course being around Laura can be a walk on the strange side of life. Josiah, youngest of the children, has actually had to live with Laura for longer than almost any of the others, and he has been around her during her young adult years more than anyone. He says, "it seems like time works differently for her. She's 28, but acts like a young teenager. It helps me understand contentedness, especially as it relates to social relationships. She doesn't take offense easily or stay hurt long. Her strength is in forgiving and being ready to accept and take people for what they are. Sometimes things are like water off a duck's back in a way. It's very hard to keep her in a normal conversation of the family. She just engages long enough to throw off a few clichés or movie lines and then she's done."

Boy, does she know those movie and TV lines! She can quote famous lines from *It's a Wonderful Life* ("you used to be so cocky!" or "my mouth's bleedin' Bert!"), John Wayne movies ("that's pretty bold talk for a one-eyed fat man" or "You're too good to give a chance to..."), *Princess Bride* (Hello, my name is Inigo Montoya...", *Get Smart* ("missed it by *that* much"; "And...loving it!"), *Hogan's Heroes* ("I know *nothing!*), *Monk*, and a host of other shows we have seen as a family. If you hear Laura talk about someone "breaking her stride" or hear her say "it's my style," or "I'd rather shower with a bear," you can bet she picked up the line from some commercial or TV show or movie. To understand how her brain works it's instructive to ask her questions and hear her responses.

Gwynne has given her Bible studies to guide her in reading God's word. Some of her answers are, how do you put it, quirky? For example, when asked about a certain passage, "What could God be teaching you through this verse?" Laura's response was, "God is your answer to your profile case that Jesus is teaching you." In another study from Psalm 65, answering the same question, she wrote "God is teaching Timothy and

I not to break our stride even when things go wrong. God is there to protect us even if we don't know each other." Sometimes when you see her answers to these questions you wonder how in the world she functions at all.

Her mind certainly runs along a different track from ours. We were on a mission trip to Idaho when Laura was seventeen, having a time of worship and sharing, when one of our young men said he just felt like God was going to do something amazing for us all on this journey north. Laura's immediate comment was to the younger kids, that "tomorrow was another day and another chance to go swimming, so don't give up hope."

There certainly are some missing pieces in her jigsaw puzzle. On that same trip some youth told a riddle, "There was a cowboy who rode out of town on Friday, was gone three days, and came back on Friday. How did he do that?" (Obvious answer is the horse's name was Friday). Here is Laura's version of the same joke that she posed for her mother, "There was a man who rode out of town on a Friday, and stayed three weeks. How did he do that?" Well...where do you begin to answer *that* riddle?

Here's another Laura original. The actual riddle says "A man goes out in the rain without a hat, umbrella, or any kind of covering, but his hair doesn't get wet. Why?" (Because he is bald) Laura's version is a bit harder to respond to. "A man went out into the rain without a hat, umbrella, or any kind of covering. Why is the man bald?" (She shrugs her shoulders and walks off). So as you can see, it's never a boring conversation when Laura gets in on it. Confusing maybe, but not boring.

And she never lets a chance to speak go by unattended. Like all our children, Laura was raised in church. We were there so often that Laura was and is *very* comfortable among Christian people. (As an aside, we have to give credit to the men of our church for giving Laura the ability to take teasing and give it right back; nothing you can say to her gets her off balance). Anyway, Laura is comfortable in church settings. So never ask the group if anyone has anything to share unless you want to hear her speak, because she *never* lets that slide without saying something. Just one of countless examples occurred when Laura was sixteen. In a prayer meeting the leader asked for prayer concerns. Laura of course raised her hand, and when called upon she said the group needed to pray for her teacher, who was having knee surgery. Gwynne happened to know that the teacher had not had knee surgery and was not contemplating knee surgery. Gwynne shifted uncomfortably as the leader made one final call for prayer requests and Laura again raised her hand. "We need to pray for my mom because she's been having pain in her back and, you know..." Given our history of having babies, Gwynne just knew that everyone suspected another one on the way, so she blushed deeply and told Laura that was enough prayer concerns for one day.

An entire book could be written about Laura's "loose cannon" problem, but we'll finish with just two more examples. Gwynne was visiting with a fellow teacher at Hedley School one day at lunch and Laura happened to be sitting with them. With no context and at a totally random moment Laura blurted out "My mom's always glad when my dad leaves for work." Gwynne was mortified and wondered what in the world her co-worker would think. But that example pales in comparison to the time Gwynne and Laura went to a shower for Rachel at her church in Sunray. Gwynne had never met the room full of ladies before, so she wanted to leave a favorable impression. Well, she and Laura left an impression alright. Laura, again at a random point in the proceedings, said in a loud voice, "My mom spanks my dad, and my dad spanks my mom." Now I want to assure you the reader that mutual adult spanking has never occurred in the Howard house for any reason. How do you even respond to such an accusation brought by one of your own children among a crowd of strangers who could not know Laura's history of random neural firings? At least at our church everyone would have thought, "Oh there goes Laura again." These folks were unaware of her proclivity for outrageous claims.

Like we said before, living with Laura is a walk on the strange side of life. Barbara Johnson is famous for saying, "Stick a geranium in your hat and be happy."[113] Laura might become famous for saying *"Enjoy your 3-week trip on Friday, and don't walk backward because you are nervous, because we're going swimming tomorrow after we solve our high profile case and we won't break our stride even if we don't know each other. And one more thing, you are God's gift to me, and that is God's gift to you."*

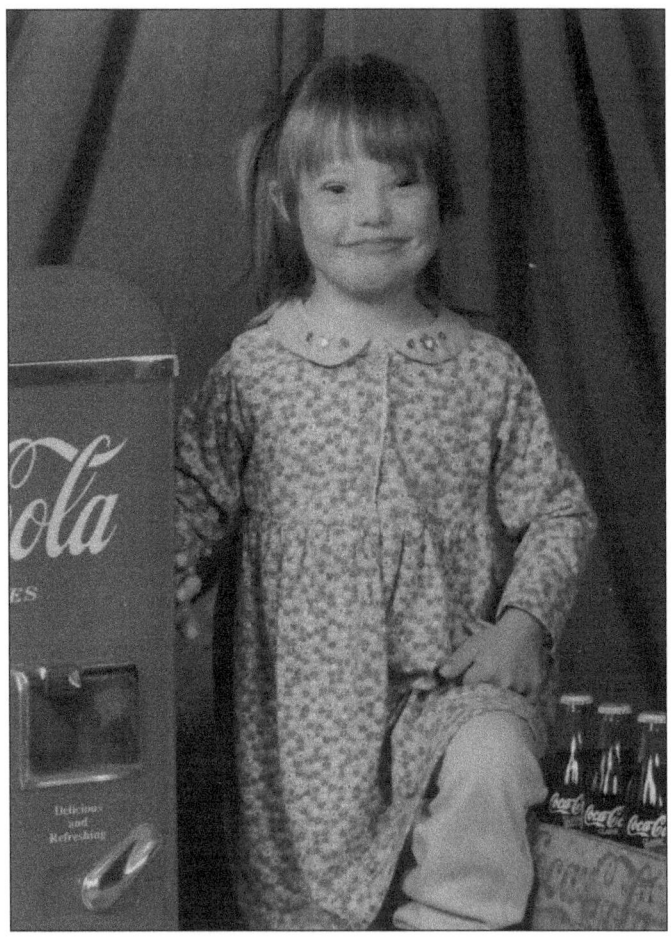

Laura Howard

Chapter Ten—Lighter Moments

Two beautiful ladies

Final Reflections

"Go to the ant, you sluggard! Consider her ways, and be wise..." (Proverbs 6:6) The wise Solomon had a good idea. He observed the world around him and reflected on it, because it taught him important lessons about life and about the God who created it. Over the 40+ years of teaching, preaching, and ministry to a wide variety of age groups, I've been asked at times where I get my ideas for sermons or sermon illustrations. My answer I think would be like Solomon's—from everywhere!

I've preached about weeds and seeds and flowers and trees, about animal behavior and cell biology and moons, planets and stars. I've preached about athletes and scholars and ranchers and teachers and doctors and nurses and linemen and farmers. I've used illustrations from the lives of historical figures and those still living that I read about in a book or article. I've highlighted the diligence of some and the ignorance or foolishness or lack of character in others, including myself and my students and children. In short, the buzzing life around us is filled with examples of worthy behavior and despicable behavior, of noble deeds and cowardly, of biblical philosophies and vain philosophies. Jesus was a master storyteller, using the familiar physical world around His listeners to make spiritual truths come alive. I seek to imitate Him in this.

Nothing in life is worthless if it teaches us something we need to know about God and His ways. Success and failure therefore are both instructive and helpful. I have often noted that when a difficulty comes into the life of a person, they can moan and groan their way through it, or they can learn from it. The great thing about being a preacher is that no matter what happens, at least you can glean a sermon illustration from it, so the situation is not wasted. The whole world around us is our instruction book if we will just take the time to reflect on it. When you look into a mirror or a still pool of water, you see yourself and think about what you see. Scripture itself is like a mirror as well, and when we see ourselves in it, we understand more fully what we really are, and as importantly, what we are to be. When we turn away we tend to forget these lessons, so it is important for us to continually look into this mirror, learn, and then act on what we learn. (James 1:23-24) It is the doer of the Word and work that is blessed. Only by reflecting on our world, ourselves, and our duties to God and man, can we live the kind of lives that honor our Creator.

Chapter Ten—Lighter Moments

Born to teach

Endnotes

1   https://www.quotetab.com/quotes/by-ruth-rendell/.
2   Reply to Loyal Colored People of Baltimore upon Presentation of a Bible on September 7, 1864 (Collected Works of Abraham Lincoln VII:542).
3   https://www.chicagotribune.com/news/ct-xpm-1990-03-18-9001230543-story.html.
4   https://benjaminspall.com/lincoln-quotes/#success/.
5   https://www.nbcnews.com/politics/congress/it-was-setup-pelosi-snips-salon-publicized-her-rule-violating-n1239139/.
6   https://wisdomquotes.org/work.php.
7   https://quoteinvestigator.com/2017/12/22/postage/.
8   https://www.gobankingrates.com/net-worth/sports/pro-athletes-lost-millions-dollars/.
9   https://www.inc.com/kevin-daum/37-quotes-from-thomas-edison-that-will-bring-out-your-best/.
10 Seth Davis, Wooden (New York: Times Books Henry Holt and Company LLC, 2014), p. 8.
11 https://www.merriam-webster.com.
12 https://www.bbc.com/news/world-asia-india-42815483/.
13 https://www.merriam-webster.com.
14 https://www.brainyquote.com/quotes/winston_churchill_124653/.

15 https://people.smu.edu/krygiel/2013/09/17/.
16 https://www.washingtonpost.com/world/asia_pacific/typhoon-vamco-manila-damage-flooding/2020/11/12/.
17 https://antimaximalist.com/comeback-stories/.
18 https://www.heart-valve-surgery.com/heart-surgery-blog/2010/03/10/first-heart-lung-machine-dewall-lillihei/.
19 https://www.acs.org/content/dam/acsorg/education/whatischemistry/landmarks/landinstantphotography/edwin-land-polaroid-booklet.pdf.
20 https://www.goodreads.com/work/quotes/903474/.
21 Flint Whitlock, The Fighting First (Boulder, CO: Westview Press), p. 200.
22 https://www.brainyquote.com/quotes/vince_lombardi_380768/.
23 https://www.goodreads.com/author/quotes/6188.Georg_Wilhelm_Friedrich_Hegel/.
24 Ron Chernow, Washington, A Life (New York: The Penguin Press, 2010), pp. 316-321.
25 https://www.brainyquote.com/quotes/ernest_hemingway_152939.
26 https://founders.archives.gov/documents/Adams/99-02-02-5162.
27 https://founders.archives.gov/documents/Adams/99-02-02-5166.
28 https://archive.nytimes.com/www.nytimes.com/books/99/07/04/specials/hemingway-obit.
29 Joe Wheeler, Abraham Lincoln—A Man of Faith and Courage (New York: Howard Books, a division of Simon and Schuster, 2008), pp. 92-95.
30 https://www.goodreads.com/quotes/34281.
31 https://www.history.com/topics/american-civil-war/stonewall-jackson/.

32 Wheeler, Lincoln, p. 75.

33 Ibid., 204-208.

34 https://www.biography.com/crime-figure/charles-pretty-boy-floyd/.

35 Gene O. Smith, Lee and Grant (Norwalk, CT: The Easton Press, 1984), p. 300.

36 Ibid., 304

37 Stephen E. Ambrose, D-Day—June 6, 1944: The Climactic Battle of World War II (New York: Simon and Schuster, 1994), pp. 178-190.

38 https://ww2days.com/medical-air-evac-plane-lost-over-albania-2.html.

39 Smith, Lee and Grant, 10-19.

40 https://www.smithsonianmag.com/history/making-sense-of-robert-e-lee-85017563/.

41 https://www.defensemedianetwork.com/stories/the-u-s-world-war-ii-troop-replacement-policy/.

42 https://nationalinterest.org/blog/the-buzz/nazi-germanys-biggest-d-day-mistakes-20849/.

43 Larry Alexander, Biggest Brother: The Life of Major Dick Winters, the Man Who Led the Band of Brothers (New York: Penguin Books, 2006), p. 105.

44 Chernow, Washington, 262.

45 Ibid., 268.

46 https://saportareport.com/the-boys-of-currahee-they-stood-alone-part-1/archived-columnists/jamils-georgia/nge/.

47 https://www.warhistoryonline.com/instant-articles/e-company-band-of-brothers.html/.

48 https://www.goodreads.com/quotes/70071-rommel-you-magnificent-bastard-i-read-your-book/.

49 https://www.goodreads.com/quotes/17976/.

50 https://blog.xbradtc.com/2016/02/the-unvarnished-truth-about-captain-herbert-sobel-marcus-brotherton/.

51 https://www.historynet.com/the-full-monty.htm.

52 https://www.reddit.com/r/TheGrittyPast/comments/90wzba/god_forgave_me_for_the_war_wwii/.

53 https://blog.rebellionresearch.com/blog/was-bismarck-a-failure/.

54 https://www.ziglar.com/articles/if-you-aim-at-nothing-2/.

55 https://www.encyclopedia.com/humanities/encyclopedias-almanacs-transcripts-and-maps/berry-raymond/.

56 https://www.republic-online.com/opinion/columns/expect-to-win-if-you-want-to-succeed/article_b74bd64c-ddff-11eb-9253-fb8a8f6601b1.html

57 https://www.trinityschoolnc.org/uploaded/Articles/The_Education_of_Abraham_Lincoln.pdf.

58 https://quod.lib.umich.edu/l/lincoln/lincoln7/1:1184/.

59 Paul Fussell, Wartime: Understanding and Behavior in the Second World War (Oxford, England: Oxford University Press, 1989), p. 282.

60 https://www.spurgeon.org/resource-library/sermons/inward-conflicts/.

61 https://www.cnn.com/2012/01/25/health/weight-loss-profile-bryan-ganey/index.html.

62 Marcus Brotherton, We Who Are Alive and Remain—Untold Stories from The Band of Brothers (New York: Berkley Publishing, 2009), pp. 45-46.

63 https://www.okbu.edu/news/2019/11/jeremy-and-caleb-freeman-deliver-inspirational-chapel-message/.

64 http://www.michaelmedved.com/.

65 https://footballfoundation.org/hof_scholars.aspx?hof=869/.

66 https://timelessbasketball.com/stuff-good-basketball-players-should-know-dick-devenzio/.

67 https://www.dailycamera.com/2009/08/14/sandrock-adams-the-master-of-masters/.

68 Daniel Defoe, Robinson Crusoe (New York: Aerie Books, Ltd., 1969), pp. 153-154.

69 https://www.brainyquote.com/quotes/john_kenneth_galbraith_122383/.

70 https://www.nytimes.com/2021/04/27/science/face-mask-guidelines-timeline.html.

71 https://apnews.com/article/fact-checking-970830023526/.

72 https://www.cnbc.com/2020/05/15/people-staying-home-can-get-covid-19/.

73 https://www.nature.com/articles/d41586-020-03141-3/.

74 https://www.timesofisrael.com/side-effects-feared-from-vaccine-are-more-common-in-covid-cases-israeli-study/.

75 https://www.nature.com/articles/d41586-021-00251-4/.

76 https://medium.com/@joschabach/flattening-the-curve-is-a-deadly-delusion/.

77 https://www.today.com/food/how-can-you-dine-out-while-wearing-mask-experts-weigh-t180420/.

78 https://www.nytimes.com/2020/05/25/us/politics/coronavirus-red-blue-states.html.

79 https://www.brainyquote.com/quotes/aesop_109735/.

80 https://www.brainyquote.com/quotes/doug_larson_107313#/.

81 https://www.goodreads.com/quotes/415646/.

82 https://www.brainyquote.com/quotes/texas_guinan_312085/.

83 https://www.goodreads.com/quotes/575351/.

84 https://www.forbes.com/quotes/7024/.

85 https://www.quotes.net/quote/16818/.

86 https://www.brainyquote.com/quotes/clarence_darrow_107296/.

87 https://www.adamsmithworks.org/documents/self-interest-rightly-understood/.
88 https://www.jstor.org/stable/25072635.
89 https://www.jstor.org/stable/pdf/2485740.pdf.
90 https://www.mdpi.com/2077-1444/9/4/118.
91 https://www.jstor.org/stable/43280930.
92 https://www.aei.org/carpe-diem/thanksgiving-lessons-about-the-failures-of-socialism-and-the-success-of-private-property-and-capitalism/.
93 https://graves.house.gov/media-center/e-newsletters/republic-if-you-can-keep-it#/.
94 https://www.thesaurus.com/browse/dedicated/.
95 https://www.investopedia.com/terms/c/copyright.asp/.
96 https://www.karwansaraypublishers.com/awblog/the-roman-conquest-of-iberia-logistics-and-supply-difficulties/.
97 https://www.goodreads.com/quotes/247269/.
98 https://www1.cbn.com/700club/dr-laura-schlessinger-caring-husbands.
99 https://blog.nationalarchives.gov.uk/remembering-city-benares-tragedy/.
100 https://magicmastsandsturdyships.weebly.com/six-small-boys-in-a-lifeboat---the-story-of-the-city-of-benares.html.
101 https://winstonchurchill.org/publications/finest-hour/finest-hour-131/woods-corner-remembering-the-ss-city-of-benares/.
102 https://www.smithsonianmag.com/history/how-almost-everyone-failed-prepare-pearl-harbor-1-180961144/.
103 https://www.gilderlehrman.org/sites/default/files/inline-pdfs/.
104 https://hymnary.org/text/this_is_my_fathers_world/.
105 https://www.goodreads.com/quotes/6313163/.
106 https://www.realcartips.com/carloans/403/.

107 https://joinyaa.com/guides/how-do-car-dealerships-make-money/.

108 https://greensboro.com/news/more-subtle-meaning-of-holiness-is-separate/article_015758/.

109 https://www.goodreads.com/quotes/422142/.

110 https://medium.com/@henry.murphy/can-you-put-in-what-god-left-out-6ddebca53459/.

111 https://voice.dts.edu/article/the-weight-of-glory-mark-l-bailey/.

112 https://www.quotes.net/mquote/841870.

113 https://www.scribd.com/book/170451005/Stick-a-Geranium-in-Your-Hat-and-Be-Happy.

CPSIA information can be obtained
at www.ICGtesting.com
Printed in the USA
LVHW091744160222
711304LV00015B/168